I0088558

THE
DISCIPLER
— TEACHER'S GUIDE —

PASTOR PAUL LEACOCK

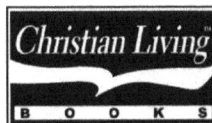

Christian Living
B O O K S

Largo, Maryland
USA

Copyright © 2019 Paul Leacock

All rights reserved under the international copyright law. No part of this book may be reproduced or transmitted in any form or by any means, electronic or mechanical, including photocopying, recording, or by any information storage and retrieval system, without the express, written permission of the author or the publisher. The exception is reviewers, who may quote brief passages in a review.

Christian Living Books, Inc.
P. O. Box 7584
Largo, MD 20792
christianlivingbooks.com
We bring your dreams to fruition.

ISBN 9781562293758

Unless otherwise marked, all Scripture quotations are taken from the New King James Version ©. Copyright © 1982 by Thomas Nelson. Used by permission. All rights reserved.

CONTENTS

DEFINING DISCIPLESHIP

DELINEATING DISCIPLESHIP

DEVELOPING DISCIPLES

DEFINING DISCIPLESHIP

1. INTRODUCTION

Welcome to the study of discipleship. It is the beginning of your walk with Christ. This study is designed in a very conscious and practical way to introduce you to what it means to be a faithful follower of Jesus Christ in your personal life, your church, your community, and society in general.

This study primarily targets new believers. However, mature believers who are new members in the assemblies where this study is offered will find fresh new insights into biblical principles. Such principles may have been previously taught but not fully explained and understood.

Additionally, the format of the study provides for group interaction so that increased learning is inevitable. Moreover, if you want to gain deeper knowledge of any one topic discussed, you can go to the suggestions for Further Study found at the end of each unit. This extends beyond the classroom and encourages the personal pursuit of biblical knowledge.

Because the desire for further study is self-motivated, it is encouraged and facilitated in every unit of this book to promote the mindset each disciple must have in pursuit of the life of Jesus. Such a mindset is not confined to specific formal studies – however well designed and executed. Rather, it is the holy habit of all who will walk in a blessed way before the Lord, meditating on His Law, day and night, until we see Him face-to-face.

It would be the highest honor to hear Him say, "Well done, good and faithful servant… enter into the joy of your lord" (Matthew 25:21). So then, "Be diligent to present yourself approved to God, a worker who does not need to be ashamed, rightly dividing the word of truth." (2 Timothy 2:15)

2. THE DISCIPLER: TEACHER'S GUIDE

Write the name of your church

_____

"Where membership is a program of discipleship"

STEPS TO FOLLOW (FOR STUDENTS)

STEP 1
- Review – The ABCs of Salvation
- Complete handouts

STEP 2
- Attend new members orientation
- Complete membership documents
- Return completed handouts

STEP 3
- Complete discipleship (new member) classes
- Complete and submit assignments prior to class

STEP 4
- Receive the right hand of fellowship

STEP 5
- Register for other discipleship classes
- Join and serve in a ministry of the church

STEP 6
- FRANgelize-Evangelize your Friends, Relatives, Associates, and Neighbors for Christ

He who has begun a good work in you will complete it. (Philippians 1:6)

Christian Discipleship is a theologically sound mentoring process that thoroughly transforms mere believers into ardent followers of Jesus Christ.

An understanding of Christian discipleship will enhance our appreciation of the subject. Hopefully, this will lead to serious application of the principles taught. Consequently, we will all become better disciples of Christ in our daily lives. In practical terms, this means we will learn and live out those essential principles, which Jesus Himself taught to His apostles and to whom He gave that Great Commission:

> All authority has been given to me in heaven and on earth. Go therefore and make disciples of all the nations, baptizing them in the name of the Father and of the Son and of the Holy Spirit, teaching them to observe all things whatever I have commanded you; and behold, I am with you always, even to the end of the age. Amen. (Matthew: 28:18-20)

The heart of that Commission is to "make disciples." The challenge arising from that is getting all believers involved in "teaching them to observe all things whatever I have commanded you" as Christ stated. Therefore, we should consider it a divine imperative to have a proper grasp of what it entails. Clearly, this study of discipleship has an importance that can hardly be exaggerated.

The first step toward achieving that grasp is to understand the uniqueness of the subject of Christian discipleship. As we shall see, it is not mere cognitive learning. It is rooted in spiritual actuality. The Christian disciple is someone who has been radically changed into God's active agent to make and mature other disciples.

Some limited elaboration on the structural aspects or components of this working definition of Christian discipleship ought to prove helpful. A fuller discussion will form the subject of a future volume.

3. THEOLOGICALLY SOUND

Christian discipleship is theologically sound because it is Biblical. It is the time-honored method of passing on the message of the Scriptures and its commensurate life of faith in God from the fathers to the heirs of the gospel. This unbroken chain of spiritual training did not have its beginning in the New Testament era. Rather, it is rooted in the Old Testament. Discipleship can be clearly seen in the traditional father and son depiction of the prophet and his mentees.

In the Old Testament, protégées of Seers were called the sons of the prophet and they regarded the presiding prophet as father (2 Kings 2:1-12; 1 Samuel 10:1-12). In the New Testament, the same practice is evident in the ministry of Jesus, the Son of God, who called men to follow Him. He also instructed them to make disciples of all ethnic groups throughout the world (Matthew 4:18-22; 28:18-20).

One notable disciple of the apostles was the apostle Paul. He exemplified the tradition of transmitting the message from the elders (spiritual fathers) to their protégées (spiritual sons) as he ventured on missionary work throughout the Roman Empire (1 John 2:1, 12; 2 Timothy 1:1-7; Titus 1:1-5).

Timothy, in particular, whom Paul personally mentored, was regarded as his son in the gospel. Paul groomed him to function in his stead and recommended him to the Philippian church in a leadership capacity as the apostle's representative:

> But I trust in the Lord Jesus to send Timothy to you shortly, that I also may be encouraged when I know your state. For I have no one like-minded, who will sincerely care for your state. For all seek their own, not the things which are of Christ Jesus. But you know his proven character, that as a son with his father he served with me in the gospel. Therefore, I hope to send him at once, as soon as I see how it goes with me. But I trust in the Lord that I myself shall also come shortly. (Philippians 2:19-24)

Having become as competent in the gospel as His father in the ministry, Timothy was instructed to disciple others as he was discipled. In doing so, the process would continue in an unbroken chain of faithfulness to Christ:

> You therefore, my son, be strong in the grace that is in Christ Jesus. And the things that you have heard from me among many witnesses, commit these to faithful men who will be able to teach others also. (2 Timothy 2:1-2)

Christian discipleship, therefore, is the practice of the prophets, the Son, and, in turn, His apostles and those to whom they entrusted the gospel.

4. TEACHER-CENTERED MENTORING PROCESS

Christian discipleship is perhaps best characterized as a process of didactic communication from the teacher to the student who is being molded. In other words, it is teacher-centered mentoring. This dynamic interaction between the teacher and the student might also be characterized as the most effective method of instruction.

Unlike the modern, Western classroom lecture format, Christian discipleship is an open-ended life-on-life process. Life-on-life is a term that is used in mentoring relationships in a variety of contexts. In the context of the teacher and student, it is a proven, effective method of learning involving the teacher and the student in a reciprocal teamwork dynamic. Nevertheless, there are distinctive aspects of the life-on-life concept in respect to Christian discipleship.

Generally, in a typical classroom, the instruction process is often restricted to the interplay between the teacher and the student(s) in a given place, space, and time. However, in Christian discipleship, ideally, the students are exposed to the full life of the teacher-mentor. They are allowed and expected to learn by directly observing the teacher's life experiences. Strengths and weaknesses, successes and failure, all are learning experiences (2 Timothy 3:10).

In the ideal Christian discipleship process, the learning is more comprehensive because it goes beyond the classroom experience. Granted, such may seem risky given that teachers or mentors – however well-intentioned or principled – may let down their charges and disappoint those who look up to them. However, that very humanity is an instructive part of the discipling process from which we must not shy away. This was even true of Jesus, our ideal teacher and mentor. In His perfect humanity, the disciples observed Jesus when He was hungry, exhausted, roiling with anger, disappointed, overwhelmed, weakened, and needing help (Matthew 4:2; John 2:13-17; 4:6; Luke 17:17; 24:26).

Jesus exposed Himself to His disciples at what might be described in practical terms as "gut level" when He shared with them His agony before facing the cross: "My soul is exceedingly sorrowful, even to death" (Matthew 26:38).

Therefore, in Christian discipleship, teachers and students need not be afraid of their humanity being seen as they both grow in grace and in the knowledge of the Lord. Teachers and students, in the context of Christian discipleship, need not focus on keeping up appearances. Instead, they should strive to follow the Lord despite their situations and encourage each other to do the same. Here are some examples:

- There were shortcomings in the relationships of Job and his friends who misunderstood his suffering
- The church observed Peter's failings as he observed theirs
- There was a falling out between Paul and Barnabas, his initial mentor
- Timorous Timothy had to be encouraged and schooled by Paul, his mentor

Other lapses and failures are recorded in Scripture as lessons to be learned (Job; Matthew 26:69-75; Luke 24:36-41; Acts 12:12-16; 11:1-3; 15:36-40; Galatians 2:11-21; 2 Timothy 1:6, 7; Revelation 2-3).

By contrast, in a conventional classroom setting, the student may only observe the instructor within the period of instruction. Behaviors, views, and opinions expressed outside the confines of that classroom are not necessarily expected to be a part of the specific subject matter. For example, an instructor may extol the virtues of a planned economic system of government but practices an exploitive, capitalistic lifestyle outside the classroom in his regular daily living. The modern student is not expected to equate the two, that is, the socialist instruction and the capitalist instructor. The subject and the subject matter here are diametrically opposite, but hypocrisy will not necessarily be applied.

Exemplified by Christ

In Christian discipleship as exemplified by Christ, the instructor and the instruction are both the subject matter. In Christian discipleship, both the teacher and that which is taught in regard to principles, laws, statutes, and ordinances are critically connected. The very practice of traditions, customs, etc. become interpretive as the way they are to be lived out by the habit(s) or lifestyle of the teacher (Greek=*didaskalos*).

Hence, in Christian discipleship, the subject matter is not for mere philosophical reflection or interaction. That is why, for example, Jesus repeatedly instructed His disciples to do as He had done (John 13:12-17). Jesus, as a teacher or mentor, was always aware that He was regarded as the paradigm exemplar and so, the one who was setting the standard for such relationships.

This principle was not lost on His disciples as they, in turn, exacted the same from their followers. They always pointed their followers to the sterling example of Christ as the one to be ultimately emulated even in the worst of circumstances (Hebrews 3:1; 12:2; 1 Peter 2:21).

Synchronization Principle

Another unique feature of Christian discipleship is the principle of the synchronization of teacher and text. In demonstrating this principle, Jesus reiterated and reaffirmed the Law. However, He emphatically steered His disciples away from its aberrations as practiced by the Pharisees and scribes (Mark 7:8-13; Matthew 15:2-6). This synchronization of the text and the teacher is seen in the profound and extensive discourse of Jesus known popularly as the Sermon on the Mount.

In the Sermon on the Mount, Jesus exposed the gap between what the teachers of the Law said and how they lived or related to their disciples. In what may be better termed the Teaching on the Mount, Jesus clarified the life of Christian discipleship for His followers by His bold, punctuating declaration: "You have heard it said … but I say unto you" (Matthew 5:21, 27, 31, 33, 38, 43). Repeatedly, Jesus warned them to live as He lived and as He taught them to live — not as the world lived (Matthew 20:25-28; Luke 22:25-30).

Christian discipleship does not subscribe to the philosophy of "Do as I say but not as I do." Rather, it is the seamless, singleness of Christ's message to 'Follow Me and do as I do, and live as I live.' This is the dynamic essence of Christian discipleship. The apostle Paul expresses this dynamic truth powerfully in these words: "Imitate me, just as I also imitate Christ." (1 Corinthians 11:1)

Furthermore, Christian discipleship is not a passive classroom experience where there is a disconnection between the teacher as a lecturer and the student as a class member. Rather, Christian discipleship is a more direct life-on-life, teaching-learning, mentoring experience from a teacher to a student in a dynamic relationship of mutual accountability.

5. THOROUGH

Christian discipleship is thorough because it is a method of instruction that encompasses, not only the teaching itself but the application of what is taught. It requires a complete, careful observance of the teachings of Christ so that education, as well as training, is in view. This is implied in the original Hebrew language usage that refers to teaching and learning: *limmud* and *malmud*.[i] These Hebrew words suggest that the disciple is prodded to do what the Lord requires as the plowman goaded oxen to accomplish his task.

Similarly, a disciple is obliged to follow the life of Christ in totality and not to select the aspects he or she prefers. Such a selective mindset is contrary or antithetical; it is counterproductive to being a Christian disciple. The Christian disciple is expected to observe all that Jesus taught. This comprehensive thoroughness of practice is expressed in the Scriptures in words that show that God requires complete devotion from those who follow Him. For example, the prophet Isaiah says this:

> Bind up the testimony, seal the law among my disciples. (Isaiah 8:16)

Nothing was to be left open to whim or fancy.

Moses also showed that God required the same devotion of the children of Israel:

> You shall not add to the word which I command you, nor take from it, that you may keep the commandments of the LORD your God which I command you. (Deuteronomy 4:2)

God required that Israel keep the commandments of the Lord with diligence and thoroughness. Likewise, true disciples are to embrace with entirety, the teachings of Christ and His apostles. Precious personal enrichment is to be gained by fully appropriating all of those teachings.

Thus, the Christian disciple has no other agenda than to follow the Lord with ardent endeavor and alert eagerness of body, soul, and mind. This total commitment will lead to the realization of what God desires in the life of the disciple. The point here is the comprehensive nature of the learning process. The approach and attitude of the Christian disciple may be likened to an apprentice who learns by observing both instruction and practice, precept and example.

---

i   As one of the twelve words for teaching in the OT, *lāmad* has the idea of training as well as educating. The training aspect can be seen in the derived term for "oxgoad," *malmēd*. In Hosea 10:11 Ephraim is taught like a heifer by a yoke and goad. The Ugaritic, *lmd* means "learn/teach" and *lamādu* means "learn" in Akkadian. The principle use of this verb is illustrated in Ps 119. Here is repeated the refrain, "Teach me thy statutes" or "thy judgments" (vv. 12, 26, 64, 66, 68, 108, 124, 135, 171). At the request of king Jehoshaphat, a group of men went out and taught the book of the Law in the cities of Judah (2 Chronicles 17:7, 9). While Greek uses two different words for "to learn" (*manthanō*) and "to teach" (*didaskō*), each having its own content, goal, and methods, Hebrew uses the same root for both words because all learning and teaching is ultimately to be found in the fear of the Lord (Deuteronomy 4:10; 14:23; 17:19; 31:12, 13). To learn this is to come to terms with the will and law of God.

Cost of Discipleship

No wonder Jesus requires His disciples to carefully count the cost of pursuing Him, inclusive of a thoughtful calculation of the losses one may incur.

> Which of you intending to build a tower, does not sit down first and count the cost, whether he has enough to finish it... so likewise, whoever of you does not forsake all that he has cannot be my disciples. (Luke 14:28-33)

On the other hand, that thoughtful calculation should include consideration of the kingdom one will inherit.

> Everyone who has left houses or brothers or sisters or fathers or mothers or wives, or children or lands, for my name's sake, shall receive a hundredfold, and inherit eternal life. (Matthew 19:28-29)

Therefore, thoroughness in teaching, learning, and living the life of Christ is a principle hallmark of Christian discipleship. It transforms the mind, body, and soul (Acts 20:27; 2:42-47; 2 Timothy 2:15; 3:16).

6. TRANSFORMATIVE

Ultimately, Christian discipleship is a transformative process. This is so because it is a dynamic learning experience that significantly alters the life of the learner. The learner develops through stages of growth – from infancy to maturity, from ignorance to reasoned understanding, from incompetence to competence, from weakness to strength, from doubt and fear to courage and faith, from moral depravity to righteousness –depending on what is being taught and who is teaching and learning.

The discipleship process is complete when the disciple is able to disciple others in the same manner he or she was discipled. Paul instructed Timothy whom he discipled.

> The things that you have heard from me among many witnesses, commit these to faithful men, who will be able to teach others also. (2 Timothy 2:2)

Clearly, Timothy graduated from mentee to mentor. Such transformation is possible because Christian discipleship is a process in which an eminent teacher (*didaskalos*) intentionally expounds and exemplifies knowledge to his students or apprentice students (*mathetes*). This is done so the students are apt to emulate that teacher in word and deed, not simply share a philosophical perspective.

Consequently, Christian discipleship requires an intimate, interdependent or symbiotic relationship between the teacher imparting his cognitive and experiential knowledge and the student imbibing and replicating that knowledge to the degree that the student becomes as learned as the teacher. Jesus says:

> It is enough for a disciple that he be like his teacher, and a servant like his master. (Matthew 10:25)

This dynamic of student attaining the status of master was demonstrated in the life and witness of the apostles.

> When they saw the boldness of Peter and John, and perceived that they were uneducated and untrained men, they marveled; and they took knowledge of them, that they had been with Jesus. (Acts 4:13)

Jesus was the Master Teacher (*Talmid*) of the Law (*Torah*) and His disciples were apprentices (*talmidim*). Twelve were called into closer association with Him. They were to be trained, commissioned, and then sent out ahead of Him to do the very works He had done.

In Luke's Gospel, we have the record of Jesus commissioning His disciples thus:

> Then He called His twelve disciples together and gave them power and authority over all demons, and to cure diseases. (Luke 9:1)

Those disciples commissioned for that special task became known as "the Twelve," a name that was used repeatedly to identify the twelve apostles.

> Then he appointed twelve, that they might be with Him and that He might send them out to preach, and to have power to heal sicknesses and to cast out demons: Simon, to whom he gave the name Peter, James, the son of Zebedee, and John, the brother of James, to whom he gave the name Boanerges, that is, 'Sons of Thunder', Andrew, Phillip, Bartholomew, Matthew, Thomas, James the son of Alphaeus, Thaddeus, Simon the Canaanite; and Judas Iscariot, who also betrayed him. (Mark 3:14-19; Matthew 26:14, 20, 47; Mark 9:35)

The radical transformation of the Twelve enabled them to set out the fundamentals of the Christian church. These apostles who started out as mere "babes" in the knowledge of God were the ones who revealed the mysteries of the gospel of the kingdom of God and His Christ. The apostle Paul explains that the foundation of the church is:

> Built upon the foundation of the apostles and prophets, Jesus Christ Himself being the chief cornerstone. (Ephesians 2:20)

Female Disciples Transformed

Also transformed were the devoted, female disciples of the Lord. These devout women were mainly described as those who catered to the physical needs of Jesus and His apostles prior to His resurrection.

Luke tells us that many women were prominent in the service of Christ as He went through several villages preaching the glad tidings of the kingdom with the Twelve.

> Certain women who had been healed of evil spirits and infirmities – Mary, called Magdalene, out of whom had come seven demons, and Joanna,

the wife of Chuza, Herod's steward, and Suzanna, and many others who provided for him from their substance. (Luke 8:1-3)

However, after the resurrection of Jesus, these women were chosen to be the first to report to the apostles and the rest of the disciples that they had seen the resurrected Lord.

> It was Mary Magdalene, Joanna, Mary the mother of James, and the other women with them, who told these things to the apostles…and they did not believe them. (Luke 24:10, 11)

Later, Jesus upbraided the men to whom these women delivered the news of His resurrection for their unbelief (Luke 24:22-26).

Women were also among the 120 disciples who were in the upper room on the Day of Pentecost. They were there to experience the promised outpouring of the Holy Spirit upon all flesh, thereby, fulfilling the prophecy of Joel.

> And it shall come to pass afterward that I will pour out my Spirit on all flesh; your sons and your daughters shall prophesy… and on my maidservants I will pour out my Spirit in those days. (Joel 2:28, 29; Acts 2:18)

Thus, mere ordinary people – men and women, fishermen, and tax collectors – were transformed by the discipleship of Rabbi Jesus. They became the foundation stones of His church of which He is the Chief Cornerstone (Ephesians 2:20; 4:11; 1 Corinthians 12:28).

Transformative Pattern

In the subsequent ministries of the apostles, the same pattern of transformation was projected wherever they made disciples. At Antioch, for example, the Gentile believers of this initially "Jewish" faith, having undergone Christian discipleship instruction by Paul and Barnabas, assembled with the church.

Luke reports that:

> For a whole year they…taught a great many people. And the disciples were first called Christians in Antioch. (Acts 11:26)

Evidently, Luke is drawing attention to the fact that a tremendous transformative effect was working itself out among the early believers. The Antiochian disciples were recognized (whether respectfully or pejoratively) as followers of Christ Jesus of Nazareth, the exemplar of their faith.

Later in his writings, the apostle Paul instructed the Corinthian believers to be followers of him as he was a follower of Christ. In saying that, Paul was not claiming to be fully like Christ in every respect. What he was saying is that the character of Christ, which he exemplified, was also to be evident in those being discipled in the churches. He instructed:

> Imitate me, just as I also imitate Christ. (1 Corinthians 11:1)

In his signature epistle to the Roman believers, Paul implored them to offer up themselves as "living sacrifices" to God and not be conformed to the worldly systems around them. He encouraged them to be transformed by the renewing of their minds. As a result, he beseeched the Roman believers to seek after the good and perfect will of God (Romans 12:1-3).

This was quite a transformation for those who were previously trapped by compulsive, sinful bodily desires and whose carnal minds were at enmity with God in a culture that was utterly ungodly (Romans 1:18-32; 7:22-25; 8:7).

We may conclude, therefore, that following Christ leads to spiritual transformation — from rebel sinner to penitent believer to Christian disciple.

Conclusion

Based on the perspective on discipleship presented above, this study calls all its teachers and students to that life of faithfulness outlined, albeit in a limited way since this is an introductory study. The principles that will be taught herein form the basic foundation on which a life of discipleship may be established.

We believe that the class dynamics and the wider church fellowship will foster spiritual growth within those who submit to them. Together, these may be launching pads for discipleship in the wider church environment. Remember that Christian discipleship is the method Jesus chose to impart the most meaningful knowledge about Himself as He commanded in Matthew 28:18, 19:

- Make disciples of all nations
- Baptize them in the name of the Father, and of the Son, and of the Holy Spirit
- Teach them to observe all things which I have commanded you

The practice of Christian discipleship introduces us to God's Word, eternal life, and the operation of the Holy Spirit in our lives. The Holy Spirit will guide and nurture the Word we have received so that it is observed in our daily living and can be passed on to others we encounter.

May you study to show yourself approved unto God, a worker who does not need to be ashamed, rightly dividing the Word of Truth so that you grow in grace and in the knowledge of our Lord and Savior Jesus Christ (2 Timothy 2:15; 1 Peter 2:1-3). May we be faithful stewards of the Master as we do His will until He returns to reward us for the work He has entrusted to our hands. AMEN!

Distribute handouts to be returned to the teacher/facilitator in the next session

- The ABCs of Salvation
- Discipleship Commitment

ABCs of Salvation

(To be completed by the students)

First Things First

The message of the gospel is as simple as ABC. The ABCs, however, though elementary, form the basis for all reading and writing. For sound Christian living, it is as important to learn the essential ABCs of the gospel as it is necessary to learn the rudimentary alphabet.

Complete the following:

All are guilty of sin

1. For _____ have _____ and fall short of the glory of God (Romans 3:23).

2. _____ we like sheep have gone astray; we have turned, _____ , to his own way; and the Lord has laid on Him the iniquity of us _____ (Isaiah 53:6).

3. But we are _____ like an unclean thing, and _____ our righteousness are like filthy rags; we _____ fade as a leaf, and our iniquities, like the wind, have taken us away (Isaiah 64:6).

All are under condemnation

1. For the wrath of God is revealed from heaven against _____ ungodliness and unrighteousness of men, who suppress the truth in unrighteousness (Romans 1:18).

2. For _____ as have sinned without law will also perish without law, and _____ as have sinned in the law will be judged by the law (Romans 2:12).

3. Therefore, just as through one man sin entered the world, and death through sin, and thus death spread to _____ men, because _____ sinned (Romans 5:12).

All need to be saved

1. Repent, and let every one of you be baptized in the name of Jesus Christ for the remission of sins; and you shall receive the gift of the Holy Spirit. For the promise is to you and to your children, and to _____ who are afar off, as many as the Lord our God will call (Acts 2:38, 39).

2. I tell you no; but unless you repent you will _____ likewise perish (Luke13:3).

Believe that Jesus is your means of salvation

1. [   ] on the Lord Jesus Christ, and you will be saved, you and your household (Acts 16:31).

2. [   ], to them He gave the right to become [   ] of [   ], to those who [   ] on His name (John 1:12).

3. For God so loved the world that He gave His only begotten Son, that whoever [   ] in Him should not [   ] but have [   ] (John 3:16).

4. He who [   ] in the Son has [   ] life; and he who does not [   ] the Son shall not see life, but the wrath of God abides on him (John 3:36).

Confess your sins (confess means to agree with God that He is right and we are wrong)

1. If we [   ] our sins, He is faithful and just to forgive us our sins and to cleanse us from all unrighteousness (1 John 1:9).

2. If you [   ] with your mouth the Lord Jesus and believe in your heart that God has raised Him from the dead, you will be saved (Romans 10:9).

Call upon God for salvation

1. For whoever [   ] on the name of the [   ] shall be saved (Romans 10:13).

2. He shall [   ] upon Me, and I will answer him; I will be with him in trouble; I will deliver him and honor him. With long [   ] I will satisfy him, and show him My salvation (Psalm 91:15, 16).

◆

After reviewing the ABCs of salvation above, make a commitment/recommitment to the Lord affirming the truth of God's Word. Whenever doubts arise, review these ABCs. Memorize the Scriptures to assure yourself of God's unfailing promise to save and keep you from ever being lost again. Now, write down your commitment.

Submit the completed copy of UNIT IA to the teacher/facilitator for class for credit.

Complete and place in your workbook reminder section until you have finished the discipleship studies. You may also post it in a visible place as motivation to continue your discipleship training and growth. Submit a copy to the teacher/facilitator of your next class for credit.

MY DISCIPLESHIP COMMITMENT

This is to certify that on this _____
day of _____ *in the year of our Lord* _____
that I _____ *being of sound mind,*
contrite in heart, and resolute in faith do hereby submit my life to
the lordship of Jesus Christ. Therefore, I present my body to God
as a living sacrifice. I dedicate my soul to the worship of His name.
I submit my mind to be trained in the whole counsel of God as a
faithful disciple until I am able to rightly divide the Word of truth to
disciple others. Further, I commit my spirit to the fullness of the Holy
Spirit and promise to love the brethren, to always seek the salvation
of my household, my family, and all with whom I come into contact.
Recognizing that I am totally reliant on His mercy and grace, I do now
consent by my hand:

Signed _____ Date _____

THE CALL TO DISCIPLESHIP

SCRIPTURE FOCUS

Jesus came to Galilee, preaching the Gospel of the Kingdom of God and saying, "The time is fulfilled, and the Kingdom of God is at hand. Repent and believe in the Gospel." (Mark 1:14, 15)

PROMPTER GUIDE

In this unit of study, you will learn about the following:

1. **CALL OF THE GOSPEL**

2. **CALL TO REPENTANCE**

3. **CALL TO BELIEVE**

PART I ◆ UNIT A

THE GOSPEL MESSAGE

INTRODUCTION

Everyone who desires to be a follower of Christ and seeks to join a Christian church does so because of the good messages heard concerning Jesus from the Scriptures.

Like you, others may have heard the good news about Jesus and the love of God He exemplifies through various media: a sermon in a church setting, a televangelist, a friend, reading a book, or an article.

By whatever means, the message received was processed in your mind as the truth, and that conviction has motivated you to respond to the good news. That good news heard is called the gospel, but what is the gospel?

1. CALL OF THE GOSPEL

The word "gospel" means "glad tidings" or "good news." It refers to the story of God as proclaimed primarily by Jesus Christ, His Son, to the people of the world. Nowhere is the gospel better expressed and explained than in the Bible, especially the New Testament.

"In the New Testament it denotes the glad tidings of the kingdom of God and of the salvation through Jesus Christ to be received by faith on the basis of His expiatory death, His burial, resurrection, and ascension."[ii] Since you have responded to the gospel message, let us examine what you have heard more fully. In doing so, you may gain a more comprehensive perspective of the gospel and better apply its message to your individual life.

Read John 1:6-8; Luke 3:1-18 (cf. Matthew 4:1-17; Mark 1:1-11)

From the definition and the scriptural readings above, it is clear that the mandate of the gospel of Jesus Christ is that we "repent" and "believe" the gospel that was proclaimed to us so we may be saved by God's love and grace. This was the message John the Baptizer preached as he prepared the nation of Israel for the Messiah/Christ (the Anointed One) whom God had sent. The purpose of the Messiah was to bring salvation and deliverance to Israel, in particular, and to the rest of the world, in general (Luke 4:18, 19; John 1:29).

---

ii   Vine's Complete Expository Dictionary of the Old and New Testament Words, Thomas Nelson Publishers 1996 (pgs. 275-276)

After Jesus the Messiah was introduced by John the Baptizer, His message was the same: "Repent, and believe in the gospel" (Mark 1:15). Again, the message of the gospel calls for two principal actions on our part: repentance and belief. What do these mean? What is God asking us to do?

2. CALL TO REPENTANCE

In a literal sense, the word "repentance" means "to perceive afterwards." Therefore, it has to do with a change of mind upon reflection of one's actions in relation to another or to something.[iii]

In the context of its use in the New Testament, repentance always refers to these:

a.   A change of one's mind or purpose for the better. Almost without exception, repentance is used to signify a change from sinful living.

b.   It also refers to regret — to be sorry for a particular action, behavior, or attitude towards something in which one is deeply involved. Hence, Jesus' message to us is to change our minds with deep regret about our sinful living.

c.   Most importantly, repentance implies a complete turnaround. In other words, you do a complete about-face. It is a radical change of direction from the wrong way to the right way in order to please God. Read the story of the prodigal son in Luke 15:11-32.

Exercise to be done in class (10-15 minutes)

Divide the class into two or more groups. Each group may report on two or more of the questions below.

Answer the following questions after group discussion:

1.   What was the younger son's request and why?

2.   How do you think he felt about working on his father's estate?

3.   Where did he go and why?

4.   How did he manage the resources his father gave him?

5.   How well did he do as a result?

6.   What words in the text indicate that he repented?

7.   What actions did the Prodigal take to correct his circumstances?

8.   What was his father's response to his return?

9.   Was everyone accepting and forgiving of his change in behavior?

---

iii   Vines, Ibid, pg. 525

3. CALL TO BELIEVE

The second action Jesus requires of us is to believe or to have faith in the gospel message we have heard. To believe is "to be persuaded of and hence, to place confidence in; to trust."[iv] To believe is not merely giving mental assent to that with which we agree. Rather, it is to rely on what we heard as the truth we stand on. In other words, to believe is to have faith, to have a firm conviction that what is heard is trustworthy and true.

Notice that the one who believes may not have all the facts to fully prove what is presented. However, the hearer is fully persuaded that what is heard is the truth and merits his/her sincerest acceptance and response (Hebrews 11:1).

Therefore, when used in relation to the Word of God or the gospel of Christ, believing has three main elements:

    a. A firm conviction producing a full acknowledgment of God's revelation or truth (John 6:68)

    b. A personal surrender of one's self to God, the purveyor of the truth (Luke 1:38; Romans 6:13; James 4:7)

    c. Conduct which corresponds to such surrender (Hebrews 11:8)

The gospel is presented to us so we can believe the truth, submit ourselves to it, and conduct our lives in accordance with the message God conveys to us through His Son, Jesus Christ. Conversely, those who fail to believe the gospel will not evidence a resolute conviction in its message, and they will not demonstrate the life-changing results such faith brings. Notice that John explained these principles when he proclaimed to his audience:

> Therefore bear fruits worthy of [in keeping with] repentance... (Luke 3:8a)

Fruits are literally the outward manifestation of the inner nature of the trees on which they grow. Figuratively, our behavior is the fruit of our inner nature. Now that we have been grafted into Christ, we ought to bear new fruit reflective of His nature and Spirit and no longer that of our sinful flesh (read Romans 11:16-18; Galatians 5:16-24).

---

iv   Vines, Ibid, pg. 61

STUDENT ACTIVITIES

—PERSONAL REFLECTION—

(see additional exercise in Appendix)

Read the story of the repentant prodigal son in Luke 15:11-32. Stop for a moment and think about any sinful behavior in your life. Think about the negative effects it is causing, has caused, or may cause in your life or in the lives of your family members and friends. Crime, violence, prejudices, suffering, diseases, persecution, war, and poverty are all largely the results of sin in one form or another.

Think about how much better our lives would be if we felt genuine sorrow for the wrongs we've committed against others and ourselves and then refrained from them. Think about how enriched our lives would become if we turn away from our sins and follow Jesus faithfully. This is the intent of the gospel message. Your discipleship begins with your repentance. You cannot be a true disciple of Jesus Christ or a bona fide member of the church until you repent of your sin(s) and believe the gospel.

MEMORY GEM

For godly sorrow produces repentance leading to salvation… (2 Corinthians 7:10)

JOURNALIZE YOUR JOURNEY

Write down meaningful insights gained and what has impacted you most in this study segment.

Blessed is the man who … in His law he meditates day and night. (Psalm 1:1-2)

FOR FURTHER STUDY (OPTIONAL)

✎   Read and reflect on these texts: 2 Samuel 11, 12; Psalm 51

NOTE: Write down any questions you need clarified. Submit your questions to your teacher/class facilitator in the next session.

Exercise 1a. (student workbook)

To be completed as homework

Read the story of Zacchaeus in Luke 19:1-10.

Answer the following questions (turn in the completed copy to your teacher/class facilitator in the next class).

1. What did Zacchaeus want?
2. What hindered his desire?
3. What actions did he take to overcome his inability?
4. How did Jesus respond to Zacchaeus' efforts?
5. How did Zacchaeus respond to Jesus' request?
6. What do you suppose they discussed over their meal?
7. What was Zacchaeus' fruit of repentance?
8. How did Jesus respond to Zacchaeus' decision (fruit)?

THE CALL TO DISCIPLESHIP

SCRIPTURE FOCUS

Jesus came to Galilee, preaching the Gospel of the Kingdom of God, and saying, "The time is fulfilled, and the Kingdom of God is at hand. Repent and believe in the Gospel." (Mark 1:14, 15)

PROMPTER GUIDE

In this unit of study, you will learn about the:

1. GOSPEL OF THE KINGDOM

2. DISLOYAL SUBJECTS OF THE KINGDOM

3. HOW DID THIS COME ABOUT?

4. DIVINE INTERVENTION

5. PROCLAMATION OF THE GOSPEL OF THE KINGDOM

PART I ◆ UNIT B

THE GOSPEL OF THE KINGDOM OF GOD

INTRODUCTION: THE LORD JESUS CHRIST

The message of the gospel of the Lord Jesus Christ points us away from our sinful behaviors. At the same time, it offers us the faith to surrender to the will of a sovereign but loving God.

The submission of our lives to the rule of the God of heaven and earth is the singular most important objective of the gospel, which Jesus preached. Hence, the gospel may be properly called "The Gospel of the Kingdom of God."

1. THE GOSPEL OF THE KINGDOM

What does the "Gospel of the Kingdom" mean? The kingdom of God is the domain of God, Who is the King of heaven and earth (Psalm 95:1-5; 1 Timothy 1:17; Revelation 19:6). It refers to the sphere of His rule. In a natural sense, a kingdom is a territory or country subject to a monarch. The borders of nations are the extent of their rulers' influence according to their individual laws and systems of government.

God is sovereign over heaven and earth. His kingdom refers more specifically to His rule in the individual lives of those who are obedient to His will. That's the true strength of a kingdom — the loyalty of its subjects! The more loyal the subjects, the stronger the ruler is.

In Scripture, God is often referred to as the Lord of hosts (angelic armies). This description expresses the power of God based on the innumerable angels at His command (Psalm 24, 46:7, 11; Jeremiah 32:16-18, 33:22; Revelation 5:11; Mathew 26:53). This is not to say that God's power (unlike human authority) is dependent on angels or humanity's loyalty, but that His rule is evident and His power displayed in their obedience.

2. DISLOYAL SUBJECTS OF THE KINGDOM

Unfortunately, the people of the world are, for the most part, living in disobedience to the will of God by the sinful acts they commit constantly (Genesis 6:5, 6; Romans 3:10-18).

Worst, sinful living subjugates us to the evil control of the Devil, the 'de facto' god of this world system (2 Corinthians 4:4-5; Ephesians 2:1-2; Luke 4:6; John 12:31; 14:30; 16:11).

The Devil's insidious attempt is to usurp the rule of the Lord and to divert anyone from hearing or believing the gospel. Consequently, he lures the unbelieving away from submitting themselves to the loving rule of God. Satan desires us to worship him instead of our Creator (Isaiah 14:12-15 cf. Luke 4:5-8).

3.   HOW DID THIS COME ABOUT?

To fully appreciate the good news of the gospel, we have to learn the bad news. This requires a review of the beginning when everything was perfect. The Bible tells us in the book of Genesis (beginnings) that God made everything in heaven and earth. When He surveyed it, He declared that it was very good (Genesis 1:31). That is to say, there was no evil, sin, or wrongdoings in the whole wide world.

This may sound idealistic and unreal, but it's only because we have become so accustomed to evil, sin, and dysfunction that we have accepted the abnormal as the norm. Just as the Bible describes it, humanity once lived in a paradise in total harmony with God, the earth, the animal kingdom, and each other (read Genesis 1, 2; Psalm 24; 8; 19:1-6; 95:1-7).

The reading of the above Scriptures makes the following key truths clear:

a. God is the sovereign Creator and Ruler of the universe

b. Man's dominion was a reflection of the supreme rule and majesty of God on the earth

c. God rules over the kingdoms/nations of the earth (and the angels of heaven)

d. Man was crowned with glory and honor and placed over all the creatures of the animal kingdom — the works of God's hands (cf. Psalm 8*)

e. Man and woman were in a covenantal relationship with God and each other

f. Man was given specific instructions that demonstrated his submission to the Lord

g. The serpent (Satan, the Devil) successfully tempted man to disobey God (Revelation 12:9)

h. Man lost his dominion in the earth as a result (John 8:34)

i. The whole earth became irrevocably changed for the worst (Genesis 3:17-19)

j. Satan gained control of the kingdoms of humanity because humanity surrendered its will to his evil influence (James 1:13-16; Romans 6:16; John 8:34)

k. Those who pursue their sinful lusts in disobedience to God become the children and subjects of Satan's kingdom (John 8:44; Ephesians 2:1; 1 John 3:8a)

l.   Disobedience leads to death both physically and spiritually (Genesis 3:16, 17; Romans 6:23; Revelation 20:11-15)

m.   God will destroy Satan's evil kingdom of this world and all who remain in it (1 John 3:8a; Revelation 12; 20)

n.   Jesus came to restore the kingdom Adam lost (Romans 5:12-21;1 John 3:8b) and to offer eternal life that was lost in Eden (Genesis 3:22-24 cf. Revelation 22:1-5).

N.B.   Understanding the gospel requires that we go beneath the surface to fully appreciate the true nature of all the things about us, which we take for granted, as well as God's grace and the work of Christ to save.

*Psalm 24 shows man crowned in the earth but the Lord proclaimed as the King of Glory. How do you understand these two dynamics in the context of the kingdom of God?

4. DIVINE INTERVENTION

Satan's tyranny, coupled with the human proclivity to sin results in one dreadful possibility: utter ruin and death. To save lost humanity, God deployed His plan of salvation. God's means of intervention was to send His Son, the Lord Jesus Christ, into the world with one specific goal in mind: to restore the rule of the kingdom of God on the earth.

This is why Jesus is called the Messiah, the Christ. He is the Anointed One sent by God to proclaim the good news of salvation from sin, all manner of sickness, all types of calamities, Satan's demonic control, and most of all, death (Luke 4:18).

5. PROCLAMATION OF THE GOSPEL OF THE KINGDOM

In true regal fashion, Jesus acted as God's royal herald and preached. He proclaimed the glad tidings of God. His official declaration announced to the nation of Israel and the world that God was reasserting His rule on the earth; all are invited to return to it. Notice Jesus' attention to His mission (Luke 4:42-43; John 4:31-35).

Jesus declared that the kingdom of God was at hand (near) and that we needed to repent and believe the good news. By our repentance and belief in the gospel, we leave the kingdom of darkness and enter the kingdom of light. We repudiate the rule of Satan in our lives and accept the rule of Christ our Savior as Lord and King (Romans 10:9, 10).

Therefore, having heard the gospel message, it is your responsibility to accept the divine salvation that has been extended to you although you are completely unworthy of it. It is the simple yet profound matter of submitting yourself to the sovereign will of God. This will require much discipline and self-effacing sacrifices on your part.

The gospel is the call to discipleship. Discipleship is the recovery of a blessed relationship with God and each other, as well as deliverance at last from the tyranny of sin, the Devil, and the world.

Exercise 1b.

How far does God want the gospel proclaimed and how big does He want His kingdom to be?

Read the following Scriptures and list the places where the gospel was/is to be proclaimed in your workbooks.

Luke 4:14-21   (Galilee, Nazareth, countryside, synagogues)

Luke 4:31-37   (Capernaum environs)

Luke 4:44   (Judean synagogues)

Luke 8:1-3   (Every city and village of Israel)

Matthew 4:23-25 (Syria, Decapolis, Jerusalem, Trans-Jordan regions)

Matthew 28:18-20 (All nations, ethnic groups, languages, peoples)

Acts 1:8 (The ends of the earth —global)

STUDENT ACTIVITIES
—PERSONAL REFLECTION—

1. The gospel is the simple yet profound message of submitting yourself to the sovereign will of God. From your perspective, how true is that statement and why would you say it is true?

2. Obedience to the gospel restores our relationship with God. How would you explain that statement to a friend?

3. Obedience to the gospel restores our relationship with each other. How exactly would you say your obedience to the gospel affects your relationship with someone with whom you are out of favor?

4. The gospel brings deliverance at last from the tyranny of sin, the Devil, and the world. Can you identify how Satan is having victory with sin in the lives of several of your friends?

MEMORY GEM

Behold, the fear [reverence and respect] of the Lord, that is wisdom, and to depart from evil is understanding. (Job 28:28)

JOURNALIZE YOUR JOURNEY

Write down the meaningful insights gained and what has impacted you most in this study segment.

Blessed is the man who… in His law he meditates day and night. (Psalm 1:1-2)

FOR FURTHER STUDY (OPTIONAL)

✎ Read these Scriptures:

Romans 1:8-26; Ephesians 2:1-9; Colossians 1:1-23; Philippians 2:5-11; Revelation 4, 5.

✎ Psalm 24 shows man crowned in the earth but the Lord proclaimed as the King of Glory. How do you understand these two dynamics in the context of the Kingdom of God?

NOTE: Write down any questions you need clarified. Submit your thoughts to your teacher/ facilitator in the next class.

Exercise 1b.2.

Complete the Scriptures below. Study them to help you understand Satan's diabolical rule in the world and in the lives of those who need to be saved.

1. Whose minds the god of this age has _____, who do not believe, lest the light of the gospel of the glory of Christ, who is the image of God, should _____ on them (2 Corinthians 4:4).

2. Those by the wayside are the ones who _____; then the devil (deceiver) comes and _____ the word out of their _____ lest they should _____ (Luke 8:12).

3. You are of your _____ the _____, and the _____ of your father you want to do. He was a _____ from the beginning, and does not stand in the _____, because there is no _____ in him. When he speaks a _____, he speaks it from his own resources, for he is a _____ and the father of it (John 8:44).

4. Be sober, be vigilant; because your _____ the _____ walks about like a _____, seeking whom he may _____ (1 Peter 5:8).

5. And you He made alive, who were [   ] in
    [   ] and [   ], in which you
    once walked according to the [   ] of this world,
    according to the [   ] of the [   ]
    of the air, the [   ] who now works in the sons of
    [   ], among whom also we all once conducted ourselves
    in the [   ] of our flesh, fulfilling the desires of the flesh
    and of the [   ], and were by nature the children of
    [   ] just as the [   ] (Ephesians 2:1-3).

6. So the [   ] was cast out, that [   ], called
    the [   ] and [   ], who deceives
    the whole world; he was [   ] to the earth, and his
    [   ] were cast out with him (Revelation 12:9).

The above references paint a gloomy picture of the human condition under satanic control. It does not take much imagination to see why the world, in the decadent condition it is in, needs the gospel (Romans 3:10-18). What can you do to help destroy the evil kingdom of Satan and restore the Kingdom of God in your life and in the lives of others?

THE CALL TO DISCIPLESHIP

Repent and believe in the gospel. (Mark 1:15b)

SCRIPTURE FOCUS

Therefore let all the house of Israel know assuredly, that God has made this Jesus, whom you crucified, both Lord and Christ. (Acts 2:36)

PROMPTER GUIDE

In this unit of study, you will learn that:

1. **JESUS IS THE LORD OF SALVATION**

2. **JESUS IS LORD BY HIS RESURRECTION**

3. **JESUS IS LORD ACCORDING TO THE SCRIPTURES**

4. **JESUS AS LORD IS ESSENTIAL FOR SALVATION**

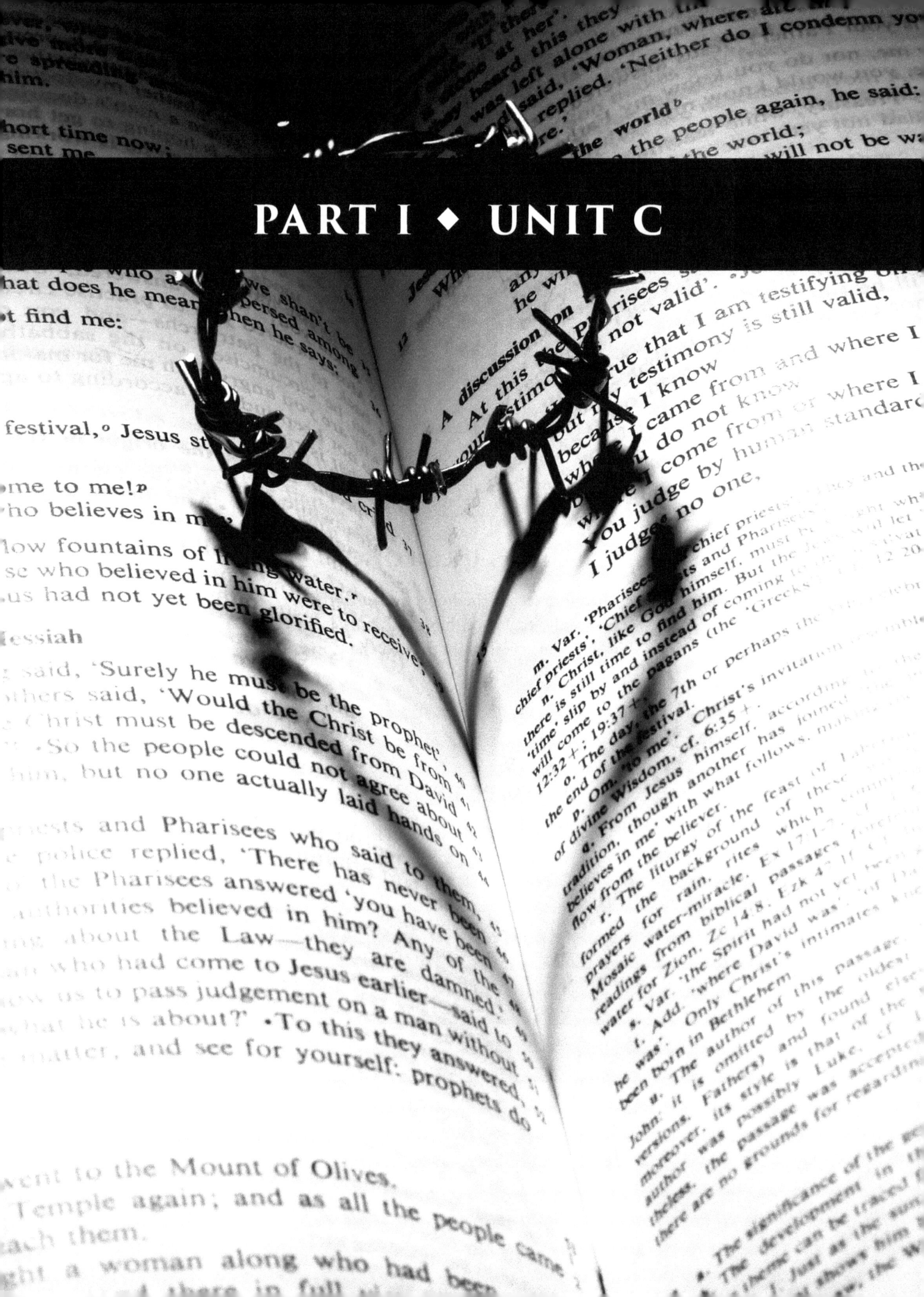

PART I ◆ UNIT C

THE GOSPEL OF THE LORD JESUS CHRIST

INTRODUCTION: THE LORD JESUS CHRIST

All persons who aspire to be true disciples need to recognize Jesus as their Lord to fully understand, experience, and proclaim the salvation that comes from God through Him. Without His Lordship, there is no Christian discipleship.

On the basis of His Lordship, Christ commissioned His disciples to be His apostles in His physical absence (Matthew 28:18, 19). In turn, they proclaimed Him Lord on the day of Pentecost (Acts 2:36).

The Lordship of Jesus continues to be the critical truth, which must be accepted by all who will receive God's salvation. He alone has the power to save lost souls (Acts 4:12). Consequently, entrance into the kingdom of God requires submission to His rule and reign (Psalm 2; Revelation 11:15; 20:1-6).

Coming to terms with the fact that Jesus is both Lord and Christ is the crux of the matter to all who would follow Him.

1. JESUS IS THE LORD OF SALVATION

It was clearly recognized that Jesus was a good man who did many "good deeds." However, salvation is not possible by simply becoming followers of a good man who did many good deeds. Peter reminded the pilgrims that they themselves had a high regard for Jesus of Nazareth. They saw Him as one who was accredited by God to the people by miracles, "wonders and signs," which God did among the people through Him (Acts 2:22). This fact was undeniable and widely known (Matthew 13:53-57; Luke 24:19).

As a matter of fact, the gospel accounts are replete with the amazing, miraculous, public works of Jesus, all of which were too numerous to record (Luke 1:1-4; John 20:30-31; 21:25). Jesus' miracles were so awesome in scope that it was evident to all but particularly to the leaders of the people that no ordinary man could perform them (John 3:1-3; Luke 4:36-42; 8:26-37; 9:37-43; 11:14-17; 13:10-17; 14:1-6; 20:1-8, 19-39; John 6:14; 11:45-54). His deeds were undeniably of God and admittedly so among His greatest detractors (John 9:16; 11:47-52;

7:30-32, 46-48). Even His words were irrefutable (Matthew 22:15-22; Mark 11:27-33; 12:34; Luke 13:15-17; 14:1-6).

However, in the same text referenced above (Acts 2:36), the apostle Peter was not offering salvation by simply following a prophet who was mighty in word and deed alone. Rather, his address to the crowd was that Jesus was Christ the LORD! The miraculous signs had indicated who He was (Luke 4:14-22). His authority over demons was particularly indicative of His divine power (Luke 9:30-36; 9:1-2; 10:1, 17-20; Matthew 12:22-28; Mark 5:1-20 cf. Acts 19:11-20).

But chief among the signs was His resurrection from the dead by His own power, the power of God (Acts 2:24; John 2:19). This is the distinguishing feat that set Jesus apart from every patriarch, prophet, priest, and king who preceded or succeeded Him in both secular and sacred history. It cemented faith in Him (Romans 1:1-5).

The resurrection of Jesus was the defining mark in the lives of the very apostles and disciples of Jesus. They now stood boldly before the throng of people asserting the preeminence of their Lord, whereas, previously, they were as doubtful and skeptical of Him as their fellow Israelites (John 20:1-9; Luke 23:13-45).

The realization of His power over death turned frightened, doubtful disciples into fearsome, dynamic men and women of faith. Thomas is the classic example of this fact. He refused to accept the testimony of his fellow disciples who were exuding with new found faith having seen the resurrected Jesus. He adamantly stated:

> Unless I see in His hands the prints of the nails, and put my finger into the print of the nails, and put my hand into His side, I will not believe. (John 20:25)

One week later, Thomas was present in the locked room with the others when Jesus came and stood in their presence. He granted Thomas' request to examine His wounds. Having done so, Thomas declared: "My Lord and my God." Jesus' response to him was just as profound (v.29). Thomas was neither rebuked for what would have been sheer blasphemy nor did Jesus disassociate Himself from his comments. Rather, Jesus acknowledged Thomas' faith in Him as his resurrected Lord.

Further, Jesus pronounced a benediction on all who will not see as Thomas did but will believe in Him as Lord (John 20:29). In his epilogue, John commends his written account to his readers confident that by believing what is written, they would have life through the name of Jesus, the Christ, the Son of God and thus, Lord (John 20:30, 31).

2. JESUS IS LORD AS SEEN BY HIS RESURRECTION

Luke, in the book of Acts – that documents the deeds of the apostles – reinforces the point of the resurrection of Jesus. He states that after Jesus' suffering, He showed Himself to His apostles and disciples for a full 40 days. Hence, He gave them convincing proof that He was indeed alive (Acts 1:1-3). This single fact was the catalyst for the dynamic ministries that turned the world "upside down" (Acts 17:6).

The apostle Paul, a former Pharisee and one who sought diligently to imprison and kill all who were followers of Jesus, recounts how he encountered the ascended Christ on the road to Damascus (Acts 9: 1-31; 22:1-8). Later, he was to concur with apostle Peter that Jesus is Lord and Christ by the resurrection from the dead.

In his pivotal letter to the church at Rome (the very nation that crucified Jesus), Paul proclaimed that Jesus the Christ, a natural descendant of David was declared by the Spirit of holiness to be the Son of God by His resurrection from the dead. Therefore, He is Jesus Christ our Lord (Romans 1:1-4). In contrast to Caesar, Jesus Christ is the true Kurios of heaven and earth.

The pronouncement that Jesus is Lord means that He is the One who has ultimate power and authority over the kingdom of God. He is the Master and Owner who has the right to dispose of anything and anyone as He chooses. Consequently, as Lord, Jesus Christ is entitled to worship and adoration. If God has made Him Lord, then it is to Him whom all must submit if they are to be saved (Philippians 2:5-11; Acts 4:8-12); this was by no means a trite claim. It brought Christians into direct conflict with the Roman Empire and every other empire that would follow.

Peter, His fellow apostles, and all the other 120 disciples of Jesus were all devout Jews and Israelites; the crowd he addressed were devout Jews and proselytes (Gentile converts to Judaism), and the occasion on which he spoke was the Feast of First Fruits. It is inconceivable that in such circumstances, they would dare to perpetrate a blasphemy at the expense of their very lives unless they truly believed it. The curious crowd could have become an angry mob.

They had seen Jesus threatened, constantly, for His assertion of equality with the Father and His ultimate death as a result (John 10:30-39; Matthew 26:63-67). The disciples knew they faced a similar fate if they were convicted of defiling such a high, holy day espousing false claims. However, they explained to the Sanhedrin who tried to restrain them from proclaiming the Lordship of Jesus Christ: "We cannot but speak the things we have seen and heard" (Acts: 4:19).

3. JESUS IS LORD ACCORDING TO THE SCRIPTURES

As Jesus did with His apostles in their unbelief and failure to understand the scriptures, the apostles, in turn, did with the amazed crowd. They expounded the Lordship of Jesus as they quoted the prophet Joel, the Psalms, and many other scriptures. Peter warned and exhorted his fellow Israelites to receive salvation through the resurrected Lord and Christ Jesus (Acts 2:40; Joel 2:28; Psalm 16:8-10). The impact of Jesus' words by the indwelling power of the Holy Spirit was incisive; it cut to their hearts so deeply they were convinced of the veracity of the facts presented to them by eyewitnesses. Spontaneously, they asked:

> Men and brethren, what shall we do? (Acts 2:37)

Without hesitation, Peter's response was given:

> Repent, and let every one of you be baptized in the name of Jesus Christ for the remission of sins. (Acts 2:38)

This was a huge requirement! Unlike prior acts of repentance and baptism, this was to be done in the name of the Lord Jesus Christ, the Messiah. That was exactly what the penitent converts in Peter's audience did. Their repentance was an admission of their powerlessness to change their sinful condition or to extricate themselves from it. They were the children of disobedience; therefore, they were under the influence of the god of this world. Only the grace of God through Jesus was able to quicken them (Ephesians 1:3-10).

Their cries of despair acknowledged their need of salvation in the name of Jesus Christ, the Lord. Their repentance and more so, their baptism in the name of the Lord Jesus Christ, signified not only their allegiance but also His Sovereign ownership; thus, His power to dispose of their sins.

In addition, repentance in the name of the Lord Jesus also signified that the converts would now be bound to and belong to Jesus Christ, the Lord just like all disciples of Christ (1 Corinthians 6:20).

4. JESUS AS LORD IS ESSENTIAL FOR SALVATION

Salvation then as it is now, requires all who wish to be saved to come under the Lordship of Jesus Christ. Therefore, all the actions, attitudes, and beliefs in our lives that are resistant to His rule must be changed. In other words, we must repent of any mindsets and reasoning that are contrary to His will and submit obediently to Him instead (2 Corinthians 10:5; Romans 12:1, 2).

Notice the disposition and attitude of the people prior to Pentecost:

- They did not believe Jesus' message (Acts 2:22)

- They apparently believed the erroneous official opinions of their leaders about Jesus (Acts 2:23)

- They had accepted the political actions of the government against Jesus even though they were unjust (Acts 2:36)

- Amazingly, we make the same mistakes

- We ignore the Word of God (the Bible) and its message

- We believe the prevailing opinions of people we hold in high regard about Jesus

- We are prepared to acknowledge Him as a good man, a philosopher, a prophet, a radical, a Rabbi etc. but never Lord of our lives and the world

- We relegate Him to the same place of insignificance and irrelevance as governments and societies do

Like the Pentecostal pilgrims, we too need to repent of our sins and wickedness and submit to the Lordship of Jesus Christ. According to the scriptures, if we confess the Lord Jesus with our mouths and if we believe in our hearts that God has raised Him from the dead, we shall be saved (Romans 10:9).

Notice that this is the same message Peter preached: accepting and believing that Jesus is the resurrected Lord. This is the truth we too need to confess. To confess (Greek = *Homologos*) in the context of the above scripture means to admit to the truth, to agree with, to acknowledge one's guilt in respect of it, and then to openly declare with the mouth that very truth, which is now embraced.

This is why receiving salvation from God is often done publicly. Peter's message was in the open before all and the response of the crowd was equally open and before all. Such public displays tend to indicate how truly serious we are about our convictions (Matthew 10:32; Revelation 3:5; cf. 2 Timothy 2:12).

After all, our sins in rebellion to God are done publicly and shamelessly. It is only fitting that our righteousness (in this case repentance) ought also to be done shamelessly before all. The Lord Jesus Himself declares:

> Therefore whoever confesses Me before men, him I will also confess before My Father who is in heaven. But whoever denies Me before men, him I will also deny before My Father who is in heaven. (Matthew 10:32, 33)

When we confess Jesus Christ as Lord, it invites the cleansing power of God through His Spirit into our lives. The scriptures declare:

> If we confess our sins, He is faithful and just to forgive us our sins and to cleanse us from all unrighteousness. (1 John 1:9)

STUDENT ACTIVITIES
—PERSONAL REFLECTION—

1. What does the concept of Lord mean to you?

2. Why did Thomas on seeing the resurrected Lord change his perception about Jesus?

3. When Thomas saw the wounds of the resurrected Lord did he put his fingers or hands into those wounds?

4. Were Thomas and the other disciples who had the privilege of seeing the resurrected Lord more blessed than us who have not seen but have believed?

MEMORY GEM

Who do men say that I am?... but who do you say that I am? (Mark 8:27- 29)

JOURNALIZE YOUR JOURNEY

Write down the meaningful insights gained and what has impacted you most in this study segment.

Blessed is the man who... in His law he meditates day and night. (Psalm 1:1-2)

FOR FURTHER STUDY (OPTIONAL)

Read these three books:

- *Who Is This King of Glory* (Tony Evans, Moody)
- *The Person of Christ* (David F. Wells, Crossway Books)
- *Jesus Divine Messiah* (Robert Reymond, Presbyterian & Reformed Publishing Co.)

NOTE: Write down any questions you need clarified. Submit them to your teacher/facilitator in your next class for helpful responses.

Exercise 1c. (Read Acts 7:54, 57-58; 8:1-3; 9:1-31)

Read the above Scriptures about Saul and answer the following questions:

1. What was Saul's view of the Jews who worshiped Jesus as Lord?
2. What role did he play in Stephen's martyrdom?
3. What role did he play in the persecution of the church?
4. How did Stephen view Jesus at the time of his death?
5. How is Saul characterized in his opposition to the church?
6. Describe Saul's response to the voice he heard?
7. How did Saul respond verbally to the voice he heard?
8. Who do you suppose he understood the speaker from heaven to be?
9. Describe Saul's change in attitude, vocabulary, and behavior after his Damascus experience.

Exercise 1c.2. (Read Matthew16:13-20)

a. What was the prevailing public opinion of Jesus?
b. Who did the disciples think Jesus was?
c. Where did Jesus say Peter's revelation came from?
d. Notice the power and authority that is bestowed on all who acknowledge Jesus Christ for who He truly is.

THE CALL TO DISCIPLESHIP

God has made this Jesus ... both Lord and Christ. (Acts 2:36)

SCRIPTURE FOCUS

"Therefore let all the house of Israel know assuredly that God has made this Jesus, whom you crucified, both Lord and Christ." Now when they heard this, they were cut to the heart, and said to Peter and the rest of the apostles, "Men and brethren, what shall we do?" Then Peter said to them, "Repent, and let every one of you be baptized in the name of Jesus Christ for the remission of sins; and you shall receive the gift of the Holy Spirit." (Acts 2:36-38)

PROMPTER GUIDE

In this unit of study, you will learn about:

1. **REPENTANCE (REVISITED)**

2. **BAPTISM (EXPOSITED)**

PART I ◆ UNIT D

THE GOSPEL OF JESUS CHRIST (GIFT OF SALVATION)

INTRODUCTION

Recall that the gospel is "good news" because it announces the love and favor of the King of heaven and earth to lost humans so that all may receive His salvation. That's the "good" in the good news. God was reestablishing His rule through His Son the Lord Jesus Christ.

Although God did not need to make a proclamation to assert His sovereignty, He chose to do so. He is sovereign over the entire universe. He is the Creator. All else is created by Him and therefore subject to His will, which He has the right to assert at any time (Psalm 24; 95; 97; 1 Timothy 1:17, Revelation 19:6).

Therefore, the proclamation of the gospel is for the benefit of those who desire to be saved from condemnation and instead, become subjects of the kingdom of heaven on earth. That's the whole point of the divine proclamation: salvation to all who would believe!

3,000 Receive Salvation!

- This was the very substance of the first gospel message Peter preached to the masses assembled in Jerusalem to celebrate the Feast of the Passover as commissioned by the ascended Jesus. The Jewish pilgrims who heard the gospel message were "cut to the heart" (Acts 2:37). In other words, they were deeply convicted because they had doubted the following truths:

- Jesus who was crucified was, indeed, both Lord and Christ

- His death on the cross was by divine providence for their sins, not His own

- His resurrection from the dead by the power of God the Father validated His Sonship

- They needed to be saved from the corruption of their time

- The outpouring of the Spirit of God comes through Christ alone

In other words, the long-awaited Messiah had come and the long desired promise of salvation was now possible through His death and resurrection to all who believe.

Previously, this was not their mindset. They did not accept Jesus as the Messiah; they were still looking for another. They were followers of the tradition of the existing religious leaders and no doubt believed the propaganda about Jesus (Matthew 28:11-15; 27:1, 20, 24, 41-43).

Realizing they were living lives displeasing to God, those who had previously rejected Jesus were now ready to receive and confess Him as their Lord. Therefore, they asked the crucial question we too need to ask: "Brothers what shall we do?" Peter's answer was swift. It was the same that Jesus and John had given, and it is still the same:

> "Repent, and let every one of you be baptized in the name of Jesus Christ for the remission of sins; and you shall receive the gift of the Holy Spirit. For the promise is to you and to your children, and to all who are afar off, as many as the Lord our God will call." And with many other words he testified and exhorted them, saying, "Be saved from this perverse generation." (Acts 2:38-40)

Notice that Peter's answer showed what his listeners were to "do" as an appropriate response to God's gracious offer of salvation in the face of gross transgression. They were called to repent and be baptized. Let us discuss these two admonitions. The first was previously discussed but will be further developed here; the second will be introduced.

1.   REPENTANCE (REVISITED)

First, there must be repentance (discussed in UNIT I Part A), but it must be in the name of Jesus Christ.

On the day of Pentecost, the Jews who heard the gospel changed their minds upon reflection of their sinful behavior. They came to the realization that their actions in relation to Jesus Christ were wrong. They were truly repentant; they were sorry for their sin of unbelief as reflected in the writer's observation. "They were cut to the heart." In an about-face, they accepted the gospel preached as the truth and were willing to do whatever was required of them. Their actions demonstrated genuine repentance.

✐   Genuine repentance moves us to do what's right

Theirs is the attitude we ought to have if we are sincerely seeking salvation through Jesus Christ and are willing with equal contrition to do what God requires of us. Notice that Peter indicated to these early converts that new life through the Holy Spirit was not only for those present on the day of Pentecost but to their descendants and to all who were afar off — that includes us. God's salvation is available to us. If we believe, we will receive life through His name.

✦ Genuine repentance moves us to faith in the gospel

Therefore, receiving the salvation of God is a matter of faith in the gospel on our part. Faith (Greek = *pistis*) means to be fully persuaded in one's mind that what is heard is the truth. Consequently, the believer acts upon it. Therefore, as the text above indicates, our believing the gospel of salvation will involve our sincere confession with our very mouths that Jesus is Lord as the gospel proclaims.

✦ Genuine repentance motivates us to ask to be saved

It is as simple as calling out to God to save us. By entreating God to rescue us, we demonstrate that we are unable to help ourselves and need Him to deliver us from our plight (Acts 2:20-21).

✦ Genuine repentance is more than feeling sorrow or remorse

Repentance for the Jerusalem pilgrims translated simply into acknowledging and accepting Jesus as Savior and Lord. After presenting convincing facts, testifying, and exhorting the listeners, Peter's conclusion was clear:

Repent and be baptized in the name of the Lord Jesus.

2. BAPTISM (EXPOSITED)

The second action Peter told the penitent believers they needed to take was that of baptism in the name of Jesus Christ. Baptism is a public, unabashed declaration of our desire to be disciples of Jesus Christ. Unlike some of our modern-day methods of baptizing converts such as in a semi-private, indoor pool at a worship service, baptism then, was a very public display. It demonstrated one's decision to radically change one's sinful lifestyle and the need for salvation. This was a serious admission to make before one's family, friends, neighbors, and even enemies. This open admission also meant that from that point on, the believers were committed to following the beliefs and teachings/teacher to which they were baptized.

a. Baptism Demonstrated

The baptism of the 3,000 converts by the apostles on the day of Pentecost was a profound step to take for those pious Jews on that high and holy day. This was particularly so since the nation and its leadership had previously rejected Jesus as the Messiah. Remember that the audience was made up of devout Jews, not just curious onlookers swayed by a persuasive message from esteemed leaders of the people. Rather, it was made up of ardent students of the scriptures and faithful adherents of the Law and the practice of their faith as they understood it. Their devotion was the exact reason why they had traveled from the remote regions of the Greco-Roman world to Jerusalem for the Feast of Pentecost.

Therefore, the instant decision of 3,000 "devout" Jews to be baptized by the apostles of Jesus (despised by the leaders of the people) was a remarkable demonstration of faith in the gospel. That must have been an impressive spectacle as that large group of new converts was publicly immersed in the name of Jesus, confessing Him as the Messiah.

As new believers in Jesus Christ, we too need to be baptized. However, because a full understanding of the significance of Christian baptism may be an unfamiliar, foreign concept to some, it may be good to pause here and understand its true significance. As a result, we may be better able to comply with the command with full appreciation and commitment. Of course, it will not be possible to give a comprehensive treatment of the entire subject of baptism here, but a concise discussion of the principal aspects of the subject will suffice our study and secure our obedience.

b.   Baptism Defined

The very word 'baptize' is a direct derivative from the original language (Greek = *baptizo*) into the English text. It means to immerse, to dip (from the action involved in the dyeing of a garment).

Significance of Baptism

Given that definition, it is easier to see its importance.

✎   Not a means of salvation alone

Baptism does not save in and of itself no more than walking through the Red Sea guaranteed arriving in the Promised Land (1 Corinthians 10:1-5). However, coupled with faith in Christ, it does bring us into the ark of safety by the grace of God (1 Peter 3:18-22).

✎   Act of consecration from sin

Baptism is an act of cleansing or consecration toward God. Sin defiles and pollutes our lives rendering us spiritually unclean. This unclean spiritual condition makes us unfit to be in a relationship with God who is holy. He does not accept sin in His presence (Isaiah 59:1-2; Hosea 1-7; Leviticus 20:23).

Consequently, sin separates the sinner from God relationally in his/her lifetime and ultimately, it will separate him/her eternally from God through death (Revelation 20:11-15, 21:8; Luke 13:24-27). Remember sin represents rebellion against God's divine rule and a transgression of His law. Several scriptural examples show the separation of God and humanity because of sin. Let us review them:

1.   Cain departs the presence of God

Then the Lord said to Cain, "Where is Abel, your brother?" He said, "I do not know. Am I my brother's keeper?" And He said, "What have you done? The voice of your brother's blood cries out to me from the ground. So now you are cursed from the earth, which has opened its mouth to receive your brother's blood from your hand. When you till the ground, it shall no longer yield its strength to you. A fugitive and a vagabond you shall be on the earth." And Cain said to the Lord, "My punishment is greater than I can bear! Surely you have driven me out this day from the face of the ground; I shall be hidden from your face; I shall be a fugitive and a vagabond on the earth, and it will happen that anyone who finds me will kill me." And the Lord said to him, "Therefore, whoever kills Cain, vengeance shall be taken on him sevenfold." And the Lord set a mark on Cain, lest anyone finding him should kill him. Then Cain went out from the presence of the Lord and dwelt in the land of Nod on the East of Eden. (Genesis 4:9-16)

2.   God's change of heart regarding humanity

Now it came to pass, when men began to multiply on the face of the earth, and daughters were born to them, that the sons of God saw the daughters of men, that they were beautiful; and they took wives for themselves of all whom they chose. And the Lord said, "My Spirit shall not strive with man forever, for he is indeed flesh; yet his days shall be one hundred and twenty years." There were giants also on the earth in those days, and also afterward, when the sons of God came in to the daughters of men and they bore children to them. Those were the mighty men who were of old, men of renown. Then the Lord saw that the wickedness of man was great in the earth, and that every intent of the thoughts of his heart was only evil continually. And the Lord was sorry that He had made man on the earth, and He was grieved in His heart. So the Lord said, "I will destroy man whom I have created from the face of the earth, both man and beast, creeping thing and birds of the air, for I am sorry that I have made them." But Noah found grace in the eyes of the Lord. (Genesis 6:1-8)

3.   God's judgment of Sodom and Gomorrah

But the men of Sodom were exceedingly wicked and sinful against the Lord ... And the Lord said, "Because the outcry against Sodom and Gomorrah is great, and because their sin is very grave ... Then the men said to Lot, "Have you anyone else here? Son-in-law, your sons, your daughters, and whomever you have in the city – take them out of this place! For we will destroy this place, because the outcry against them has grown great before the face of the Lord, and the Lord has sent us to destroy it." (Genesis 13:13; 18:20; 19:12, 13, 24, 25 cf. 2 Peter 2:7)

4.   Sin is a spiritual barrier

Behold, the Lord's hand is not shortened, that it cannot save; nor His ear heavy, that it cannot hear. But your iniquities have separated you from your God; And your sins have hidden His face from you, so that He will not hear. For your hands are defiled with blood, and your fingers with iniquity; Your lips have spoken lies, your tongue has muttered perversity. (Isaiah 59:1-3)

5.   Sin is repulsive in nature

You meet him who rejoices and does righteousness, who remembers You in Your ways. You are indeed angry, for we have sinned - in these ways we continue; and we need to be saved. But we are all like an unclean thing, and all our righteousness are like filthy rags; we all fade as a leaf, and our iniquities, like the wind, have taken us away. (Isaiah 64:5, 6 cf. Ezekiel 36:25)

6.   Sin defiles hands and hearts

Therefore submit to God. Resist the devil and he will flee from you. Draw near to God and He will draw near to you. Cleanse your hands, you sinners; and purify your hearts, you double-minded ... Let your laughter be turned to mourning and your joy to gloom. (James 4:7-9)

7.   Sin must be cleansed

Notice that in all of these scriptures, there is a recurring theme: sin, which has polluted the sinners and the earth itself.

Also notice that in the scriptures used above, cleansing is needed to address the unclean conditions identified:

- Hands that are filled with blood
- Defiled fingers
- Lips sullied by lies
- Tongues coated with perversity
- Filthy rags of self- righteousness
- Lives likened to unclean things
- Impure hearts

Sin separates a holy God from sinful humanity; hence, there is a consequential need for cleansing if that separation is to be bridged.

8.   Baptism, the means of cleansing

Baptism demonstrates this spiritual cleansing that purifies the mind. The ritual of purification was instituted by the Lord, Himself, under Moses to preserve the relationship of Israel with Himself. Hyssop, as well as the fingers of the priests, and even a clean bird were dipped (baptized) in blood, water, and oil to purify people as well as materials (Leviticus 4:17-20; 14:1-9; 16-18; 34-51; Numbers 19:16-18).

The Hebrew word in its verb form *tābal* (dip, plunge) conveys the meaning of the immersion of one item into another: bread in vinegar (Ruth 2:14), feet in water (Joshua 3:15), a coat in blood (Genesis 37:31). The Greek word *baptō* is the common Septuagint (LXX)[v] rendering of this root.

"Dipping" is employed in Israel's religious ritual of cleansing (see 1 Samuel 14:27 for dipping in the common, literal sense). In the sin offering, whereby the sinner's (individual or national) iniquity is atoned, the priest dips his fingers into the blood of the sacrificial animal and sprinkles it before the veil or places it upon the altar's horns (Leviticus 4:6, 17; 9:9).[vi]

9. Baptism identifies the sinner with the sacrifice (Hebrews 9:19-22 cf. John 13:1-11)

But the argument can be made, and rightly so, that water cannot cleanse a person from his/her sins since water is a physical element and sin a spiritual condition. However, the point is not necessarily the water itself, but what the use of the water as a cleansing agent does and what that act of obedience means to God, as well as the unclean sinner.

In the rite of purification, for example, the repentant sinner was identified with the sacrificial animal's blood, which is shed as a representation of the death paid for the sin. The writer of Hebrews draws on this figure of cleansing by blood showing that there was no remission of sins without it (Hebrews 9:19-22). Similarly, blood was placed on the doorposts at Passover, representing the lamb's blood, which is shed substitutionally for the firstborn (Exodus 12:22).

Identification of the unclean with the sacrifice for cleansing is also conveyed in the cleansing ritual for lepers and the dead (Leviticus 14:6, 16, 51; 2 Kings 5:14; Numbers 19:18). Hyssop, or the priest's finger, was dipped in water or oil (cleansing agents) and sprinkled upon the unclean object to identify it as cleansed.[vii]

Nevertheless, water cleanses. It has inherent properties that clean and purify. We use water to wash our hands so they can be clean, especially before meals. We wash our clothes with water. It is also used in a multiplicity of ways as a solvent to eliminate impurities or to dilute concentrated solutions that may be harmful.

Furthermore, while water is the physical agent, cleansing is the spiritual state that is achieved by its application. The fact is that in each action of cleansing, there is an accompanying inner act of cleaning of one's self from the sin(s) that defiles. The inner act of cleansing involves the change of mind in respect of sin, the loss of desire for sin, and the reverence of God and His Law instead of self. These will all constitute purification as one repudiates and divorces one's self from the defilement of sinful behavior.

---

v   The Septuagint Version of The Old Testament in Greek
vi   Harris, Robert Laird; Archer, Gleason Leonard; Waltke, Bruce K.: Theological Wordbook of the Old Testament. electronic ed. Chicago: Moody Press, 1999, c 1980, S.
vii   Ibid

Therefore, cleansing, which baptism conveys, is the spiritual act that addresses the spiritual uncleanness caused by sin. As a result of the use of water as specified by God, the unholy becomes holy and acceptable to God who is perfectly holy.

c.   Biblical Historical Cleansing

Baptism is often only seen as a New Testament concept. However, as an act of cleansing and consecration, it may also be traced throughout the Old Testament. A review of it may reinforce our understanding and help us appreciate Jesus' mandate to all who will follow Him (Matthew 28:19).

Consecration by Water

God instructed Moses to consecrate the people of Israel so they may stand clean before Him at Sinai:

> Go to the people and consecrate them today and tomorrow, and let them wash their clothes ... So Moses went down from the mountain to the people and sanctified the people, and they washed their clothes. (Exodus 19:10, 14)

Having done according to God's requirement of cleansing by water, the people were fit to meet with God:

> And Moses brought the people out of the camp to meet with God, and they stood at the foot of the mountain. (Exodus 19:17)

Rite of Purification (the putting away of defilement)

The Israelites were required to maintain purity in themselves, household vessels, and dwellings, as well as places and utensils of worship. This was necessary for them to remain in relationship with God and each other in the community. Hence, God instituted a rite of purification by water (Numbers 19). The rite of purification separated the clean from the unclean and the pure from the impure. Failure to purify one's self with the water of purification was a capital offense punishable by death.

> But the man who is unclean and does not purify himself, that person shall be cut off from among the assembly, because he has defiled the sanctuary of the Lord. The water of purification has not been sprinkled on him; he is unclean. (Numbers 19:20)

For his own sin, King David prayed:

> Wash me thoroughly from my iniquity, and cleanse from my sin ... Purge me with hyssop, and I shall be clean; wash me and I shall be whiter than snow. (Psalm 51:2, 7)

His immoral actions had sullied his character and resulted in adultery and manslaughter from which he needed cleansing.

Subsequently, to an erring nation that has backslidden, Isaiah warns,

> Wash yourselves, make yourselves clean; put away the evil of your doings from before my eyes. Cease to do evil. (Isaiah 1:16)

God makes this prophetic pronouncement to a disobedient nation in exile for defiling the land of Israel:

> For I will take you from among the nations, gather you out of all countries, and bring you into your own land. Then I will sprinkle clean water on you, and you shall be clean; I will cleanse you from all your filthiness and from all your idols. I will give you a new heart and put a new spirit within you; I will take the heart of stone out of your flesh and give you a heart of flesh. I will put My Spirit within you and cause you to walk in My statutes, and you will keep My judgments and do them. Then you shall dwell in the land that I give to your fathers; you shall be My people and I will be your God. I will deliver you from all your uncleannesses. (Ezekiel 36:24-29a)

Notice that commensurate with the sprinkling is the cessation of idolatrous worship, which is considered filthiness. A new heart and spirit are necessary to replace the old heart marred by idolatry.

What a fitting prophetic picture that parallels Peter's sermon to the Jews of the diaspora scattered throughout the Roman Empire who had gathered in Jerusalem for Pentecost. In fulfillment of Ezekiel's prophecy, Peter invited them back to restore their relationship with their Lord whom they had rejected. But for them to be so accepted, they had to be cleansed by the purifying water of baptism. To those who complied, Peter confirmed the prophetic outcome: God will give His Holy Spirit to live within them.

Concurring with this divine dispensation to repentant Jews, Paul testifies that at his conversion, he was similarly told by Ananias:

> And now why are you waiting? Arise and be baptized, and wash away your sins, calling on the name of the Lord. (Acts 22:16)

Paul, as well as his fellow Israelite converts, understood that cleansing and consecration were essential parts of appropriating the salvation of Christ in a time of grace and favor introduced by the gospel as prophesied in Scripture (Acts 3:19; cf. Matthew 3:1-8).

Thus, elsewhere in several of his epistles, Paul employed this same concept of cleansing in the lives of those who were in relationship or those whom he exhorted to be in relationship with God.

Therefore, having these promises, beloved, let us cleanse ourselves from all filthiness of the flesh and spirit, perfecting holiness in the fear of God. (2 Corinthians 7:1)

d. Baptism, a Spiritual Cleansing

Now that we have a Biblical view of consecration as represented by baptism, it may be helpful to also consider the deeper spiritual cleansing, which baptism represents.

✎   Symbolic of the Cleansing by the Word of God

Water baptism conveys a deeper sense of cleansing. It is more than an initial, singular act of consecration. It conveys a sense of cleansing the entire life by the application of the truth of the Word of God. It is indicative of the purification of the mind and heart defiled by evil thoughts and lustful desires. Unlike immersion in water, which is an initial, singular act of consecration, the Word of God is a continual cleanser, which keeps the inner life pure.

Consequently, the Scriptures declare:

There is also an antitype which now saves us -baptism (not the removal of the filth of the flesh, but the answer of a good conscience toward God), through the resurrection of Jesus Christ. (1 Peter 3:21)

How can a young man cleanse his way? By taking heed according to your word. (Psalm 119:9)

Husbands love your wives just as Christ also loved the Church and gave Himself for her, that He might sanctify and cleanse her with the washing of water by the word, that He might present her to Himself a glorious church, not having spot or wrinkle or any such thing, but that she should be holy and without blemish. (Ephesians 5:25-27)

You are already clean because of the word which I have spoken to you. (John 15:3)

Sanctify them by your truth. Your word is truth. (John 17:17)

Therefore lay aside all filthiness and overflow of wickedness, and receive with meekness the implanted word, which is able to save your souls. But be doers of the word, and not hearers only, deceiving yourselves. (James 1:21, 22)

✎   Symbolic of the Cleansing Blood of Jesus

Perhaps of greatest importance, water baptism is very representative of the cleansing of sin through the blood of Jesus Christ. Water primarily cleanses the body; the Word of God purifies the mind. However, the true detergent for sin-stained lives is the blood of the

Lamb. As filthy garments are cleansed by a solution of water to remove their stains, we are thoroughly cleansed by the blood of Jesus for the physical and spiritual removal of all sin (1 John 1:8, 9).

The blood of Jesus is certainly efficacious, but because this cleansing is spiritual and therefore, less perceptible, it may be better conveyed to our understanding through our senses in the act of baptism. The language and symbolism of cleansing by blood is consistently deployed in discussing this phenomenon by the writers of Scripture in the same way it was used of water:

> But Christ came as High Priest of the good things to come, with the greater and more perfect tabernacle not made with hands, that is, not of this creation. Not with the blood of goats and calves, but with His own blood He entered the Most Holy Place once for all, having obtained eternal redemption. For if the blood of bulls and goats and the ashes of a heifer, sprinkling the unclean, sanctifies for the purifying of the flesh, how much more shall the blood of Christ, who through the eternal Spirit offered Himself without spot to God, cleanse your conscience from dead works to serve the living God? (Hebrews 9:11-14)

> But if we walk in the light as He is in the light, we have fellowship with one another, and the blood of Jesus Christ His Son cleanses us from all sin. (1 John 1:7)

> Grace to you and peace from Him who is and who was and who is to come, and from the seven Spirits who are before His throne, and from Jesus Christ, the faithful witness, the firstborn from the dead, and the ruler over the kings of the earth. To Him who loved us and washed us from our sins in His own blood (Revelation 1:4, 5)

> Then one of the elders answered, saying to me, "Who are these arrayed in white robes, and where did they come from?" And I said to him, "Sir, you know." So he said to me, "These are the ones who come out of the great tribulation, and washed their robes and made them white in the blood of the Lamb. (Revelation 7:13, 14)

Earlier in our definition of baptism, we indicated that it harkens back to the immersing of garments in dyes. The makers of fine garments dipped the clothing of their clients into their color solutions to beautify them. Especially when they were dipped in red/scarlet, they were irrevocably changed.

Similarly, when we are baptized as sincere believers calling upon the name of the Lord for salvation, we are spiritually baptized in the blood of Christ to be irrevocably changed from sinners to saints. God's Word states,

Though your sins are like scarlet, they shall be as white as snow; though they are red like crimson, they shall be as wool. (Isaiah 1:18b)

To Him who loved us and washed us from our sins in His own blood, and has made us kings and priests to His God and Father, to Him be glory and dominion forever and ever. Amen. (Revelation 1:5b, 6)

To the ... elect according to the foreknowledge of God the Father, in sanctification of the Spirit, for obedience and sprinkling of the blood of Jesus Christ. (1 Peter 1:1-2)

In Him we have redemption through His blood, the forgiveness of sins, according to the riches of His grace. (Ephesians 1:7)

✎   Symbolic of the Cleansing by the Spirit

The Holy Spirit will be given more attention in subsequent sessions. It is sufficient to say at this point, however, that water baptism is also symbolic of the spiritual cleansing and filling of the believer's life by the Holy Spirit. This is also referred to as the baptism of the Spirit (Ezekiel 36:24-29; Mark 1:8; Acts 1:5, 19:1-6; 1 Corinthians 12:13; Galatians 3:27).

STUDENT ACTIVITIES
—PERSONAL REFLECTION—

1. How important is baptism in your discipleship process?

2. What parts of the body are recommended for cleansing in the scriptures above?

3. How does the writer recommend those parts of the body be cleansed?

4. What importance does God put on cleanliness?

5. You have heard the saying, "Cleanliness is next to godliness." What do you suppose it means?

MEMORY GEM

And now why are you waiting? Arise and be baptized, and wash away your sins, calling on the name of the Lord. (Acts 22:16)

JOURNALIZE YOUR JOURNEY

Write down the meaningful insights gained and what has impacted you most in this study segment.

> Blessed is the man who… in His law he meditates day and night. (Psalm 1:1-2)

FOR FURTHER STUDY (OPTIONAL)

Review the Scriptures above on baptism as symbol of cleansing by the Word, the blood, by the Spirit. Study their contexts. Envision your need for cleansing in a very physical sense as the case for purification is presented. John, who baptized by water, declared that Jesus would baptize with fire and the Holy Ghost. What do you suppose he meant? How is baptism in Paul's teaching portrayed as a form of death (Romans 6:3-12; Colossians 2:12-15)?

NOTE: Write down any questions you need clarified. Submit them to your teacher/facilitator in the next class for helpful responses.

PART II

THE CALL TO FELLOWSHIP

They continued steadfastly in the apostles'
doctrine and fellowship. (Acts 2:42)

SCRIPTURE FOCUS

Then those who gladly received his word were baptized; and that day about three thousand souls were added to them. And they continued steadfastly in the apostles' doctrine and fellowship, in the breaking of bread, and in prayers. (Acts 2:41, 42)

PROMPTER GUIDE

In this unit of study, you will learn about the first converts to Christianity and how:

1. **THEY CONTINUED STEADFASTLY IN THE APOSTOLIC DOCTRINE**

2. **THEY CONTINUED STEADFASTLY IN THE FELLOWSHIP OF THE APOSTLES AND DISCIPLES**

3. **THEY CONTINUED STEADFASTLY IN PRAYER WITH THE APOSTLES AND DISCIPLES**

4. **THEY CONTINUED STEADFASTLY IN CORPORATE WORSHIP**

PART II ◆ UNIT A

JOINING THE CHURCH
(GREEK = *KOINONIA*)

INTRODUCTION

Joining the church is more than being among the 'saved folk' or placing your name on the church roll. To be added to the number is to become a part of the Body of Christ. In common church talk, this is referred to as being 'in fellowship'.

The idea of "fellowship" refers to the common association of persons who share the same ideas, concepts, concerns, and enterprises. The term also alludes to the participating in activities as comrades who share mutual love and personal relationships with each other. Such Christian companionship constitutes a church 'body' — the Body of Christ.

Collectively, the members become a local Christian community of disciples learning how to live lovingly toward each other. This is done under the leadership of the local and general assembly of the church members whom the apostle Paul called the saints.

> To the church of God which is at Corinth, to those who are sanctified in Christ Jesus, called to be saints, with all who in every place call upon the name of Jesus Christ our Lord. (1 Corinthians 1:2)

In order for Christian fellowship to occur, each person who joins the church needs to be discipled. Remember a disciple is an adherent, a devoted student or follower whose aim is to become like his teacher.

Thus, when we submit ourselves to sound biblical instruction among the believers, we will be transformed from our carnal selves to be conformed to the very image of Jesus Christ.

Prior to joining the church, people have divergent views, opinions, concepts, and philosophies that are markedly different from each other and certainly from that of the Bible and the church.

Thus, there needs to be a concerted effort of submission to the discipleship process which the church is mandated to provide for each new convert as presented here to you as it was to those first converts on the day of Pentecost. Let us do a further study of their discipleship process in the primary New Testament church as reported in the Acts of the Apostles.

The Case of the First Converts (Membership=Discipleship)

How did the 3,000 people who joined the assembly of the believers at Pentecost approach their membership? They realized they needed to change their views, opinions, and positions on the scriptures pertaining to Christ Jesus. Therefore, they were now ready and waiting for the apostles to enlighten them. After all, they had failed to recognize that their long-awaited Messiah had come in the person of Jesus Christ whom Israel had rejected. This was particularly damning for a Jew because the hope of all Israel rested on the Messiah as prophesied in Scripture (Genesis 3:15; 22:15-18; 49:10; Deuteronomy 18:18, 19; Psalm 2; 118:22-26; Isaiah 7:14; 9:1-7; 11:1-2; 53; 40:1-5; Jeremiah 23:5-6; Micah 5:2; Malachi 3:1-3).

Additionally, they had witnessed Jesus' miraculous works, signs, and wonders, which validated Him before Israel (Acts 2:22); yet, they had given Him over to be crucified 50 days before. Suddenly, it all made sense. He was crucified at Passover (the Lamb of God) and raised from the dead three days later (after the Paschal Sabbath) — exactly on the first day of first fruits (Christ the first fruit — begotten from the dead (1 Corinthians 15:20; Revelation 1:5). Now, exactly 50 days later on the Feast of Pentecost, there is a supernatural outpouring of the Holy Spirit. It was all too meticulous, too calculated. It fitted together too perfectly not to be divinely orchestrated as Peter had pointed out (Acts 2:22-36).

Therefore, having repented and having been baptized, they submitted themselves to the process of discipleship in key areas described as follows:

1. THEY CONTINUED STEADFASTLY IN THE APOSTOLIC DOCTRINE

Having received Jesus as Savior and Lord and having been baptized into the body of believers, the new converts "continued steadfastly" in the entire teaching program of the church. It was clear from Peter's message that there was much they needed to understand. Therefore, the new converts became thus:

- Adherents — they stuck to the apostles' teaching and instruction
- Avid — they continued faithfully in their attendance
- Ardent — they gave unremitting care to the admonition
- Audacious — they persevered in faith without fainting

N. B.   The very book of Acts, which details the account of the first converts was written to Theophilus, a student disciple of Luke. Both the gospel narrative of Luke and Acts were to ensure that Theophilus knew the certainty of those things in which he was instructed (Luke 1:1-4; Acts 1:1-3).

2. THEY CONTINUED IN THE FELLOWSHIP OF THE APOSTLES AND DISCIPLES

It is one thing to enroll in and attend a local church. It is quite another to enjoin and enjoy the fellowship of the church. To be in fellowship (Greek = koinonia) means to share in common, to be a partaker, one who contributes or communicates as a partner. Such active participation is what is alluded to in the illustration of the body; each joint is involved in the entire well-being of the body (Ephesians 4:16).

The new converts became active participants in the fellowship meetings of the Apostles. In this way, they could be instructed and made aware of the function each plays within the body of Christ. Each member's role is according to what is divinely appropriate, not what the member prefers, likes or even desires to be or do (1 Corinthians 12:1-13).

The new believers also recognized that the Apostles and the other disciples were the *disciples of Jesus*. It was upon *those followers of Jesus* that the Spirit of God came, not any others. These were the ones who fulfilled the prophecy as evidenced by their speaking in tongues and prophesying to the unbelievers (Acts 2:1-8; Joel 2: 28-29; 1 Corinthians 14:21, 22).

Hence, they knew that to understand the whole counsel of God they needed to submit themselves to those who did, i.e. the disciples of Jesus Christ led by the apostles. Therefore, they became the disciples of the apostles in the same way that the apostles had been the disciples of Jesus three years prior.

- They broke bread together – they ate together from house to house
- They had all things in common – they sold and shared their possessions
- They gave to the needy among them (Acts 2:45; 4:34-37)
- They had singleness of heart – sincerity, and simplicity
- They had joy – they were extremely jubilant and exultant

Pentecost was the feast of the first fruits at harvest time. Traditionally, this was a time of jubilation, feasting, and happiness as the Lord of the harvest and the reapers rejoiced together over the produce that was in-gathered (Exodus 23:16; 34:22). Now, at this Pentecost, the spiritual fruit was being harvested; there was joy in the city of Jerusalem as well as in heaven (Jeremiah 2:3; John 4:36; Luke 10:17-22).

3. THEY CONTINUED IN PRAYER WITH THE APOSTLES AND DISCIPLES

As a beleaguered group under the scrutiny of the leaders, it was natural for the Apostles and the disciples (the church) to pray for divine help in navigating the hostilities that were shown to Jesus who was turned over to the Romans to be crucified.

The Jewish, and no doubt, Roman leaders were watching to see if any of the disciples would make claims about His resurrection having heard the report of the soldiers who were at His tomb (Matthew 28:1-17). After all, it would have been damaging if the realization among the populace was that Jesus of Nazareth was, in fact, the Messiah being validated by His resurrection as He was known to have predicted (Mark 8:31; Luke 18:31-33).

Interestingly, the fact of Jesus' resurrection was so startling to the very disciples of Jesus that some of them demanded proof (John 20:24-29; Luke 24:10-12, 24-26), infallible proof of which, Luke states, Jesus gave "many" (Acts 1:3). This evidence emboldened the disciples to preach the Lordship of Christ after much prayer in the face of threats and intimidation (Acts 4:21-33). After prayer, the witness of the Apostles turned them from a frightful few to a fearless force of witnesses (Luke 22:55-62; Acts 4:13; 5:12-42).

It was not long before the hostilities that were leveled at Jesus would be directed to them, His followers (Acts 4:1, 2, 21; 5:21-40; 6:8-15; 7:54; 8:3; 9:1-2; 20-31; 21:27-36). Consequently, they devoted themselves to prayer in significant ways:

- They prayed as the apostles prayed (Acts 3:1; 6:4)
- They prayed in each other's houses in fellowship meetings (Acts 2:46; 12:5, 12; Romans 6:5)
- They prayed for boldness to continue witnessing (Acts 4:23-33)
- They prayed for divine assistance (Acts 4:23-33)
- They prayed for their leaders' deliverance (Acts 12:5-17)
- They prayed for the forgiveness of their persecutors as Jesus had taught them (Acts 7:59, 60; Matthew 5:43-48)

4. THEY CONTINUED IN CORPORATE WORSHIP

The motifs of the church alluded to earlier and discussed more fully in the next segment, all suggest a community of believers meeting and working together. This was different from the more western, individual approach to faith and religion with which we are more familiar. As Howard Snyder describes in his work *The Community of the King*,[viii] the church in any locale, is more than a mere collection of people who happen to share common religious interests and cultures. Snyder explains that the church community is a separate, distinct community that differs from the rest of the society from which it is drawn. Its values, central interest, and reason for being are determined by its allegiance to Christ and His teachings as relayed by His apostles and their successors throughout time.

It stands to reason then that the early church would assemble for joint worship. Theirs was unlikely to be the strict programmatic liturgies we are exposed to in the current church, but many of the elements of our liturgies are borrowed from them. The term "worship service"

---

viii   Synder, Howard A, The Community of the King, IVP, 1977

would not likely have been used. Rather, words such as thanksgiving, confession, confessing, and praising would have been more common among them.

While we may not know specifically how they did any of those expressions, we do know that the disciples expressed themselves in these forms of worship:

- They attended temple services
- They praised God
- They ate together in fellowship meals (Jude 12; 2 Peter 2:13)
- They sang psalms, hymns, and spiritual songs (Ephesians 5:19; Colossians 3:16; Acts 16:25; Hebrews 13:15)
- They read Scripture (1 Timothy 4:13; Luke 4:16; 10:26; Acts 13:15; Romans 15:4)
- They exhorted and were exhorted (Acts 17:1-2, 10, 11)

These expressions of worship were done as a collective body, not in an individual sense as is often our case today. The corporate worship of the first church was a critical factor in the growth and development of the New Testament Church that has now spawned centuries extending to our times. It is worship worthy of our emulation.

STUDENT ACTIVITIES
—PERSONAL REFLECTION—

1. How significant is your church assembly to the Lord?

2. How significant should your church assembly be to you?

3. What role did the church have in your conversion?

4. What role do you envision for yourself as a member of this church assembly?

MEMORY GEM

Now, therefore, you are no longer strangers and foreigners, but fellow citizens with the saints and members of the household of God, having been built on the foundation of the apostles and prophets, Jesus Christ Himself being the chief cornerstone, in whom the whole building, being fitted together, grows into a holy temple in the Lord, in whom you also are being built together for a dwelling place of God in the Spirit. (Ephesians 2:19-22)

JOURNALIZE YOUR JOURNEY

Write down the meaningful insights gained and what has impacted you most in this study segment.

Blessed is the man who … in his law he meditates day and night. (Psalm 1:1-2)

FOR FURTHER STUDY (OPTIONAL)

Read:

- *The Community of the King* (Howard Snyder, IVP)
- *Jesus Divine Messiah* (Robert Reymond, Presbyterian & Reformed Publishing Co.)
- Review the Hymn "The Church's One Foundation"
- Research the Nicene Creed

NOTE: Write down any questions you need clarified. Submit them to your teacher/facilitator in your next class for helpful responses.

Exercise 2a. (to be done as homework)

1. What is doctrine?
2. How important is it to know the doctrine of the apostles?
3. What is the Apostles Creed?
4. What is fellowship?
5. How do you fellowship with the church body?
6. How important is it to eat with other church members?
7. How do simplicity and sincerity play a part in good fellowship?

Exercise 2a.2.

Review the story of Ananias and Sapphira (Acts 5:1-11) and answer the following:

1. Compare Barnabas' actions to those of Ananias and Sapphira's What was similar/different?
2. Why was Peter so draconian with the couple?
3. Why do you suppose they died?
4. What lessons might we learn here?

Exercise 2a.3. (group discussion)

Review the story of Philip in Samaria (Acts 8:1-25) and discuss the following in your group:

1. Who was Simon?
2. What drew him to Philip?
3. Was he truly converted?
4. Was he added to the number?

THE CALL TO FELLOWSHIP

And the Lord added to the church daily those who were being saved. (Acts 2:47b)

SCRIPTURE FOCUS

Then those who gladly received his word were baptized; and that day about three thousand souls were added to them ... And the Lord added to the church daily those who were being saved. (Acts 2:41, 47b)

PROMPTER GUIDE

In this unit of study, you will learn about the character of the church:

1. **THE BODY OF CHRIST**

2. **THE TEMPLE OF GOD**

3. **THE FLOCK OF GOD**

4. **THE BRIDE OF CHRIST**

5. **THE CALLED OUT PEOPLE OF GOD (GREEK = *EKKLESIA*)**

PART II ◆ UNIT B

JOINING THE CHURCH FELLOWSHIP (The Body of Christ)

INTRODUCTION

It is the will of God for all who receive His Son Jesus Christ as Savior and Lord to become united in fellowship as one body, members of one another. Every new believer becomes part of the family of God by virtue of the new birth. Having then accepted the Lord Jesus Christ as Savior, it is necessary to be in fellowship with other believers.

Collectively, all believers in Jesus Christ are called the Church; they make up the body of Christ and His kingdom of God on earth. This rather mystical union has implications for the individual believer, as well as the collective body of believers. On the one hand, new members have the personal responsibility of engaging in relationships of sharing and caring. They do so by actively participating in the church assemblies they join. They also need to submit themselves to the leadership in those assemblies.

On the other hand, the church leadership has the responsibility of discipling new members helping them to fit into the structure and ministries of the local assembly. This mutual interaction has been the practice of the Christian Church from its inception and must continue to be so for the mandate of Christ to be carried out.

An understanding of the biblical structure of the Church is an essential part of the discipleship process so that each disciple has a comprehensive view of the Church's composition, function, and purpose universally.

In this discipleship segment, we will examine the descriptions of the Church given in Scripture against the backdrop of our text, which describes the birth of the Christian Church. This understanding will enable the disciple to think beyond any local/denominational trappings to see the overall mission of the Church and the part he/she is called to play in achieving it.

Believers Baptized and Added

Having accepted the message of the gospel as preached by Peter on the day of Pentecost, new believers were added to the congregation (120) of the followers of Jesus who met in the upper room that day (Acts 1:12-15). Notice that the joining of the initial 3,000 believers was not a flippant prospect to be mulled over. Instead, it was a conscientious, bold, and dramatic decision underscored by their public baptism! Their union with Jesus' followers must have been an enormous public spectacle that drew much public attention.

Remember that the new converts were "devout Jews" who had come from several nations to celebrate the Feast of Pentecost (first fruits) in Jerusalem. These were persons who were committed to their traditional faith and religious practices. Their very presence in Jerusalem, having made arduous journeys from distant lands was indicative of their reverence to God and their willingness to worship God as set out in the Law (Exodus 23:16; 34:22-23; Leviticus 23:9-21).

However, once they heard and understood the gospel of Jesus Christ, they were pricked in their hearts. On seeing their need for repentance, they united with the apostles and the saints who proclaimed that gospel. They became included in the body; they joined the church — all three thousand of them! Then more were added daily; 5,000 more were added a few days later; then the number multiplied (Acts 2:47; 4:4; 6:1). This was exponential growth that soon drew the attention and ire of the Jewish leaders and later Rome as the believers congregated and fellowshipped.

In Jerusalem, there was no Christian church building for the new believers to go into as we do in our modern edifices today. The temple was still the official place of worship of Israel. Synagogues (small sanctuaries in villages) were outposts of the temple in villages where worshipers gathered to hear Scripture read and explained. The Rabbis also taught there much the same as they do today. The upper room where the disciples of Jesus met was no more than a rented room without prior religious adornments of significance.

No wonder the Bible does not point to a place where the new believers joined but described the group joined as, the Church (assembly), to which more were added daily (Acts 2:47b). There was no established institution with formal offices of pastors, bishops, elders, ushers, or even deacons initially. All of this was to come later as the church, the assembly of Christian believers, became a more formal organization.

Nevertheless, the assembly of believers, who were followers of Jesus the Christ, and all those who accepted their message and were thereby saved (Acts 2:47) became a church body, which we call the 'early church' for distinction.

The body of Christ is the first of the descriptions, which characterizes the Church that we will study, followed by the temple of God, the flock of God, the bride of Christ, and the ekklesia of God. While they are not totally mutually exclusive, each depiction provides a unique scriptural view of the church as seen by the Lord.

These depictions help us to understand the nature and structure of the Church of Jesus Christ. They also help us to see past the veneers of form into the spiritual substance, which constitutes the church universal.

1. THE BODY OF CHRIST

The Church then, as it is now, was a body of Christian believers. Therefore, Christian believers can be called the body of Christ. The apostle Paul used this description to demonstrate the unity, function, and connectivity of individual believers to each other. The depiction of the believers as a body of related members can be found in several of the letters Paul wrote to various Christian assemblies throughout the Greco-Roman world so that they may have a proper understanding of the nature of the Church. His epistle to the Corinthians is the most extensive on the subject. He noted that the Church, like the human body, is not made up of one member but many.

Therefore, no part can be exclusive and still remain a part of the body. Moreover, no part is all that the body needs. Rather, as in a physical body, the Church is a composite, integrated system of members (parts) that are interdependent on each other. Consequently, there should be no schism (division) among members but all should have mutual care and concern for each other. If one suffers, all suffer and if one is honored, all rejoice with him (1 Corinthians 12:12-26).

Having established his premise, Paul declared,

> Now you are the body of Christ, and members individually. (1 Corinthians 12:27)

Similarly, to the Roman believers Paul wrote,

> For as we have many members in one body, but all the members do not have the same function, so we, being many, are one body in Christ, and individually members one of another. (Romans 12:4, 5)

Again, Paul upbraided the Corinthian believers who had fallen into carnal behaviors using the same motif.

> Do you not know that your bodies are members of Christ? Shall I then take the members of Christ and make them the members of a harlot? Certainly not! (1 Corinthians 6:15)

In the epistle to the Ephesians, Christ is presented as the head of the Church, His body (Ephesians 4:13-16; 5:23). This characterization is stated more pointedly in the epistle to the Colossians where Christ is portrayed as the preeminent head of the church which is described there again as His body (Colossians 1:18). This is not simply a metaphor, but a living reality of unity and integration so there is a consistency of character between Christ and His Church (Ephesians 4:13-16). Thus, the Roman saints are cautioned as were the Corinthians that since Christ is righteous, His followers are required to demonstrate a commensurate individual righteousness.

Therefore do not let sin reign in your mortal body, that you should obey it in its lusts. And do not present your members as instruments of unrighteousness to sin, but present yourselves to God as being alive from the dead, and your members as instruments of righteousness to God. (Romans 6:12, 13)

Such individual responsibility produces a collective unity and synergy of love and harmony throughout the body that matches the glorious head, Christ (Romans 12:9, 10). It also is the means by which the entire Church body grows. This is achieved by each member functioning according to the spiritual vocation to which each believer is called. It is also accomplished by each ministering to one another as designed and designated, the way healthy cells do in a physical body (Ephesians 4:11-16).

2. TEMPLE OF GOD/BUILDING

Closely aligned to the depiction of the Church as the body of Christ, is its description as the "Temple of the Living God." To fully appreciate seeing a mass of human beings as a static temple building, we may need to review briefly how temples were presented in Scripture, their significance to those who worshiped in them, and the deity worshiped. Of course, a full exposé is neither possible nor necessary here. However, a small treatment follows to help you understand the reason for this depiction of the church in Scripture.

Temples were descriptive of:

- The House of the King (Hebrew = *Hêkāl*, Temple)

This term, as commonly used within Israel, referred to the dwelling place of the king, a palace. Applied to God, hêkāl refers to the dwelling place of the great King (Ezra 3:6)[ix] whose true temple is heaven itself (Psalm 11:4; Micah 1:2; Habakkuk 2:20; Isaiah 6:1). Unlike us, God is transcendent. In other words, He is above all and over all. He is the immortal, eternal Spirit unlimited by time, space, and matter. However, He allowed physical places to facilitate worship but never to house and contain Him as was done to the gods in other religions (Exodus 20:22-26; 1 Samuel 5:2; 1 Chronicles 10:10; Jeremiah 7:9-12; Numbers 22:40).

In this respect, He accommodated David's desire to build Him a temple of worship. The Lord was sensitive to David's finite human nature, which we all share. He recognized our need for tangible things to help us perceive and better relate to the immaterial such as Himself (2 Samuel 7). Therefore, the resulting temple later known as Solomon's temple was one of such special places on earth that were dedicated to sacred worship.

---

ix   Harris, R. Laird; Archer, Gleason Leonard; Waltke, Bruce K.: Theological Wordbook of the Old Testament. electronic ed. Chicago: Moody Press, 1999, c1980, S. 215

✎　The Place of Gathering and Service

A place where God's people assembled for holy convocations and where the priest served in their religious and liturgical roles; these were, likewise, to be regarded as His "dwelling place" as well (Numbers 9:15; 3:5-7; Psalm 24; 15; 46:4; Zechariah 6:12,13; John 2:12-17; Mark 11:15-17).

✎　The Place of Worship and Encounter

The tabernacle and subsequently, the temple, were the most sacred of the places that facilitated the worship relationship between finite man and the infinite God. Even though God is everywhere and cannot be confined to a physical location on earth, He deemed it fitting to dedicate a place where His people may better focus their attention, adoration, and affection individually and collectively on Him. It is also a place where they may receive instruction to be applied to their individual lives (2 Samuel 7:4-14).

Therefore, the tabernacle/temple was always more than a place; it was a point of encounter where God met with His people and His people fellowshipped with Him individually and collectively (Exodus 25:8, 22; 1 Samuel 1:4-9).

✎　The Place of Divine Presence

The LORD'S presence was seen in such phenomenon as the glory cloud, the pillar of fire, the pot of manna, the Urim, and the Thummim, which afforded answers to those who enquired of the Lord before the priests (Exodus 13:21; 28:30; 30:1-6; Leviticus 16:20-21; 1 Samuel 28:6).

✎　Tabernacling Among Us

In the New Testament period of Jesus, however, there is a major shift in temple significance. First, the presence of God is not exhibited symbolically in the phenomenon such as a glory cloud or a column of fire, but it is veiled in the very person of the man Christ Jesus. The Gospels declare that Jesus Christ, the Son of God, is the full embodiment of the Godhead in the flesh. He is said to have tabernacled with us. His physical presence was even more glorious than that of the pillar of fire and the cloud of glory. As John expressed it,

> And the Word became flesh and dwelt among us, and we beheld His glory, the
> glory as of the only begotten of the Father, full of grace and truth. (John 1:14)

The existing physical temple of His day (Herod's Temple), no longer had the same significance; no more than a shadow has more importance than the person casting the shadow. The new temple will be a living structure. Worship was now to be done in spirit and in truth, not by location (John 4:24). Wherever two or three of the people of the Lord were gathered, His presence would be there among them. They would be the temple, not the stones and other physical materials that housed them (Matthew 18:20; 1 Corinthians 5:4; Matthew 23:38; 24:1-3).

✎   Tabernacling Within Us

More than living among us, Jesus made it clear that He would send the Holy Spirit to dwell within each believer. Thus, He would make each one an individual dwelling place (temple of God). Therefore, the indwelling of the Spirit makes the collective body of believers the composite, living, dwelling place of His Holy Spirit. Consequently, the Church is a living temple and each member living stones (2 Corinthians 6:16). Paul explained to the Ephesian believers how the spiritual house is built and constituted.

> Now, therefore, you are no longer strangers and foreigners, but fellow citizens with the saints and members of the household of God, having been built on the foundation of the apostles and prophets, Jesus Christ Himself being the chief cornerstone, in whom the whole building, being fitted together, grows into a holy temple in the Lord, in whom you also are being built together for a dwelling place of God in the Spirit. (Ephesians 2:19-22)

The new temple of worship was now a spiritual one. It was just as it is in heaven where the angels forever worship and praise the Lord most holy in the portals of glory (Revelation 4). Jesus made it clear that the time would come and "now is" when the Father would not be worshiped in specified locations, but that the true worshipers will worship the Father in spirit and in truth (John 4:21-24).

This declaration is indicative of the fact that the true temple was not a physical localized one, but a spiritual one. This reality captures the essence of the Psalms in which the writer expresses that God "inhabits the praises of Israel," His people, and signals a new kingdom reality that we must recognize.

✎   The Living Temple

The apostle Peter similarly writes of the church as a living temple in this way:

> Coming to Him as to a living stone, rejected indeed by men, but chosen by God and precious, you also, as living stones, are being built up a spiritual house, a holy priesthood, to offer up spiritual sacrifices acceptable to God through Jesus Christ. (1 Peter 2:4, 5)

Here, the Church is presented as a compact, spiritual house made up of individual living stones, believers, built upon the foundation of the apostles and prophets with Christ as the Chief Cornerstone (cf. Ephesians 2:19-20). Recall that in the building of the tabernacle and, in turn, the temple, God instructed Moses to construct these places of worship after the pattern of the one he saw in heaven (Exodus 25:9; Numbers 8:4).

Isaiah's vision of that heavenly temple depicts the Lord enthroned and the seraphim uttering unceasing praises to His holiness (Isaiah 6:1-4). The prophet is not enraptured by the awesomeness of any physical structures. Rather, he is in awe of the majesty of His Holiness and the praises rendered to Him.

In the living temple, the offerings are spiritual sacrifices of praise (1 Peter 2:6; Hebrews 13:15; Psalm 27:6; Jeremiah 33:11).

In summary, the Church is the exclusive spiritual dwelling place of the sovereign God and His Son, Jesus Christ, the King of kings and Lord of lords. It is the community in which Jesus tabernacles via His Holy Spirit who indwells each believer. Like the Israelite community overshadowed by the Shekinah glory of God, the Church is a universal union of people of every tribe, nation, language, and ethnicity where God is worshiped in spirit and in truth. The Church is the living temple of God composed of believers who are its living stones; Christ Himself being the Chief Cornerstone.

3. THE FLOCK OF GOD

Every new believer is one of God's sheep. Thus, the Church is God's flock. Numerous references in Scripture show this description. One of the best known is Psalm 23 in which the writer, David, portrays himself as a sheep in the care of the Lord his Shepherd.

Several other Psalms describe God's dealing with His people leading, feeding and caring for them (Psalm 77:20; 78:52; 80:1). They also show His peoples' acknowledgment of Him as their Shepherd (Psalm 79:13; 95:7; 100:3). Note the stern warnings which are given by the prophets from God to the leaders of Israel. He talks about under-shepherds who ill-treat His people, His sheep, whom He loves (Jeremiah 23; 50:6; Ezekiel 34; Zechariah 13:7-9; Matthew 9:36).

Jesus describes Himself as the Good Shepherd in contrast to the hirelings who do not care for the flock as He does (John 10:1-6,16; 15:13). His flock will be at His right hand when He returns in judgment (Matthew 25:32-34). Believers as God's sheep underscore what each believer means to God and how He expects them to be cared for within the Church by the pastors (shepherds) placed over their care (1 Peter 5:2; Psalm 77:20; 80:1)

4. BRIDE OF CHRIST

Just as the believers make up the flock of God, collectively, the Church is the bride of Christ. In this depiction, the deep affection and love Christ has for His people are expressed. A bride is one betrothed, engaged to be married to someone who has proposed marriage.

The scriptures describe Jesus as the beloved bridegroom and the Church as His beloved bride. It is in this relationship every new believer is included and cultivated as a pearl of great price, the apple of His eye, His beloved (Ephesians 5:21-33; Matthew 25:1-13; Revelation 22:16-21; Song of Solomon).

5. CHURCH OF GOD (GREEK = *EKKLESIA* — CALLED OUT ASSEMBLY)

Note also that joining the Church was carefully orchestrated by the Lord Himself. It was the "Lord" who added daily those who were being saved. You may have chosen to attend an assembly of believers or you may have even decided to sign up for membership. However, if you are sincerely responding to the gospel of Christ, you will recognize that the Lord was leading you all along just as He had done for the Jews on the day of Pentecost.

It is easy to understand, therefore, why the Church of Jesus Christ is called the ekklesia, the called out assembly. Through the message of the gospel preached, the call of God is made for people to repent and follow Christ, instead of the spirit of this world that controls the disobedient in their trespasses and sins (Ephesians 2:1-3). Those called out are gathered together in common worship and praise to the Lord and constitute the church locally and universally.

Like Israel who was called out of Egypt to be the people of God who gathered and worshiped Him, all who heed the call are members of:

> The general assembly and church of the firstborn who are registered in heaven, to God the Judge of all, to the spirits of just men made perfect, to Jesus the Mediator of the new covenant, and to the blood of sprinkling that speaks better things than that of Abel. (Hebrews 12:23, 24)

New believers in Christ can be described as the elect and chosen of God because it is God's initiation that makes salvation possible. It is God who constantly presents the gospel through various means to ensure it is heard and heeded. Without nullifying the free will of those who hear the gospel, it is God who actually draws sinners to His light from the darkness where they hide because of sin, shame, guilt, and fear.

The phenomenal act of God's calling is clearly demonstrated in the way Jesus directed His disciples to target the pilgrims at Pentecost. Jesus was very insistent that His disciples waited in Jerusalem until the day of the outpouring of the Holy Spirit. He foreknew that those who had come to the city of Jerusalem for the Feast of Pentecost would hear the gospel and heed it. These were devout Jews from 18 geographic locations! Those who responded to Peter's sermon were now able to return with the gospel they embraced to share in their countries of residence. Thereby, the gospel message was strategically spread.

Notice that these pilgrims were descendants of Abraham and their Gentile converts. Hence, they were already those God promised to save (Genesis 12:1-3).

Like them, each believer ought to be grateful that he/she has been given the privilege to be elected of God and chosen to be among the brethren of His dear Son (Romans 8:28-30).

The foregoing metaphors are the scriptural description of the Church. There are universal and transcend the denominational or specific doctrinal or worship traditions of the various organizations that describe themselves as Christian churches and to which we belong. However, we all need to exercise care what church groups we join to ensure that these concepts are taught and practiced.

In our present age, there are myriads of religious traditions and practices that have sprung up and have taken root over the centuries since the day of Pentecost when Peter preached (AD33). Therefore, it is critically important, that you understand what you mean to God. You are a member of the body of Christ, a living stone of His Temple, a sheep of His pasture, His Son's bride. You are His called out assembly chosen and elect from among the peoples of the world through the gospel you have come to believe.

STUDENT ACTIVITIES
—PERSONAL REFLECTION—

Each disciple is groomed to live out faith in a specific sociological and religious context. Therefore, it is important that attention is paid to the structure and culture of the specific assembly/denomination you choose to join. This is so you may become a part of the brethren in compliance with the particular rules and regulations that govern the church. This is no different from what happened in the early Church. As it grew in scope and size, various principles and practices were put in place as Scripture and the leading of the Holy Spirit allowed (Acts 6; 11:19-30; 15).

As new assemblies were planted throughout the Greco-Roman world, epistles were written with spiritual and temporal instructions so that the membership lived in harmony without inviting any blasphemy to the name of Christ. Matters such as idolatry, eating foods offered to idols, sexual behaviors, marriage, family, circumcision, the Holy Spirit, governmental authority, master and slave relationships and a myriad of other issues were all addressed in the epistles of the apostles and their designates.

We are privileged to have these writings to guide our current assemblies, especially those in peculiar circumstances. Care must be taken to learn the manners of your church context so as to be a vital part of the body of Christ there.

Reflect on the Hymn: "The Church's One Foundation" (Samuel J Stone; Samuel Wesley)

The Church's One Foundation

The church's one foundation is Jesus Christ her Lord; she is his new creation by water and the Word. From heaven he came and sought her to be his holy bride; with his own blood he bought her, and for her life he died.

Elect from every nation, yet one o'er all the earth; her charter of salvation, one Lord, one faith, one birth; one holy name she blesses, partakes one holy food, and to one hope she presses, with every grace endued.

Though with a scornful wonder we see her sore oppressed, by schisms rent asunder, by heresies distressed, yet saints their watch are keeping; their cry goes up, "How long?" And soon the night of weeping shall be the morn of song.

Mid toil and tribulation, and tumult of her war, she waits the consummation of peace forevermore; till, with the vision glorious, her longing eyes are blest, and the great church victorious shall be the church at rest.

Yet she on earth hath union with God the Three in One, and mystic sweet communion with those whose rest is won. O happy ones and holy! Lord, give us grace that we like them, the meek and lowly, on high may dwell with thee.

Answer the following questions:

1. What images studied do you see in the first stanza?

2. According to the second stanza, how is the church composed?

3. How is the unity of the church hinted in the same stanza?

4. According to the third stanza, what are the two threats to the church's unity?

> ## MEMORY GEM
>
> Now, therefore, you are no longer strangers and foreigners, but fellow citizens with the saints and members of the household of God, having been built on the foundation of the apostles and prophets, Jesus Christ Himself being the chief cornerstone, in whom the whole building, being fitted together, grows into a holy temple in the Lord, in whom you also are being built together for a dwelling place of God in the Spirit. (Ephesians 2:19-22)

JOURNALIZE YOUR JOURNEY

Write down the meaningful insights gained and what has impacted you most in this study segment.

> Blessed is the man who… in His law he meditates day and night. (Psalm 1:1-2)

FOR FURTHER STUDY (Optional)

- ✎ Meditate on Revelation 1-3
- ✎ Read *The Church in the Bible and the in World*, Carson D.A., Wipf & Stock Publishers

NOTE: Write down any questions you need clarified. Submit them to your teacher/facilitator in the next class for helpful responses.

THE CALL TO FELLOWSHIP

You shall receive the gift of the Holy Spirit (Acts 2:38b).

SCRIPTURE FOCUS

And you shall receive the gift of the Holy Spirit. For the promise is to you and to your children, and to all who are afar off, as many as the Lord our God will call. (Acts 2:38b,39)

Therefore being exalted to the right hand of God, and having received from the Father the promise of the Holy Spirit, He poured out this which you now see and hear. (Acts 2:33)

PROMPTER GUIDE

In this unit of study, you will learn about:

1. **OUTPOURING OF THE HOLY SPIRIT**

2. **THE GIFT OF THE HOLY SPIRIT- THE SPIRIT OF GOD**

3. **THE DAY OF THE LORD- AT PENTECOST?**

4. **THE HAND OF THE LORD**

PART II ◆ UNIT C

THE GIFT OF THE HOLY SPIRIT

INTRODUCTION

Earlier in our study, we examined the principal thrust of Peter's charismatic message — Jesus Christ is Lord! We also learned that submission to His lordship evidenced by repentance and baptism is necessary for our salvation. More importantly, however, Peter also declared that those who repent and are baptized in the name of the Lord Jesus will receive the "gift of the Holy Spirit." He was reminding his fellow Israelites and the Gentile converts to Judaism that the charismata of the Holy Spirit is exactly what God had promised to bestow on all flesh — those present, their children, and all those who are afar off, "…as many as the Lord our God will call" (Acts 2:39).

These words are as significant to us today as there were to those present in the primary Pentecostal audience. What was apparent to them that day was prophetic and foretold what needs to be a present reality in our lives today — the receiving of the gift of God's grace in the person of the Holy Spirit. He is God's promise to us as well. We are "those who were afar off" (Ephesians 2:11-14; Romans 10:11-13). We are among the "many" whom the Lord our God has called to salvation (Ephesians 4:1-7).

In order for us to appreciate the immeasurable worth of the gift of the Holy Spirit and the gifts He bestows, we need to review its immeasurable value to those on whom it was first bestowed at Pentecost and then to subsequent believers in the New Testament church.

1. THE OUTPOURING OF THE HOLY SPIRIT — A TIME OF REFRESHING

Recall that the crowd had heard a cacophony of languages that were supernaturally spoken by mere Galileans who, for the most part, were uneducated and therefore unlearned in other languages. The crowd was composed of Parthians, Medes, Elamites, Mesopotamians, Judeans, Cappadocians, Pontians, Asians, Pamphylians, Egyptians, Libyans, Romans, Cretans, and Arabians. Therefore, those from these areas recognized that it was a sign of great significance, but of what exactly? Some in their haste tried to brush off the phenomenon as a fluke by suggesting the apostles and disciples were intoxicated with too much wine. This was a foolish, illogical explanation since excessive alcohol consumption impairs speech; it does not enable it.

It was clear that the apostles and disciples, males and females, were not babbling incoherent gibberish as drunkards would. Rather, their intelligible speech was clearly understood. Indeed, each people group present heard their distinct native dialektos (dialects). They admitted:

> We hear them speaking in our own tongues the wonderful works of God.
> (Acts 2:11)

Obviously, they were speaking established languages (Greek = *glossolalia*) by some supernatural means!

To clarify the confusion, Peter stood up and explained that the phenomenon witnessed was not the absurd result of drunkenness, but rather, the absolute fulfillment of the outpouring of the Holy Spirit as prophesied by Joel (Acts 2: 17-21 cf. Joel 2:28-32). This outpouring of the Holy Spirit was the grace of God, which they received when they repented and were baptized in the name of the Lord Jesus Christ. This brings up the question then: what is this gift of the Holy Spirit?

2. THE GIFT OF THE HOLY SPIRIT — THE SPIRIT OF GOD

Peter's audience understood that the Holy Spirit was a reference to the Spirit of God as seen in the Old Testament. To receive the Holy Spirit was to be endowed with the abiding presence and power of God in one's life. For the people of Israel, no gift was greater! Every priest, prophet, and king was anointed as a sign that he functioned under the aegis and authority of the Spirit of God.

Throughout biblical history, the Spirit of God was operative in the lives of the patriarchs, prophets, priests, and other outstanding leaders (1 Samuel 10:6; 16:13; 2 Kings 2:5; Judges 3:10; 6:34; 11:29; 13:25; 14:6). For example, Moses and Aaron were enabled to perform mighty plagues upon Egypt to break its power and control over her Hebrew slaves whom God wanted freed (Numbers 11:17, 24-29).

Via the same Spirit, Aaron and his sons were anointed to intercede between God and the nation of Israel (Exodus 29:41-46 cf. Hebrews 9:1-10). The judges who led Israel in her formative years as a nation knew the triumph of reliance on the Holy Spirit and the tragedy of non-reliance (Judges 3:10; 6:34; 11:29; 13:25; 14:6, 19; 16:20; Psalm 51:11, 12).

Later, the kings who ruled over the unified nation were endowed with the Holy Spirit in order to govern successfully (1 Samuel 10:1; 11:6, 7; 16:13). The absence of the Spirit of God meant abject failure (1 Samuel 18:1-12; 28:6; Psalm 51:11).

Of course, the largest body of references to the significance of the Holy Spirit in the life of the nation is seen in the ministry of the prophets and in their prophetic writings (Isaiah 11:1-2; 32: 15; 63:10, 11, 14; Ezekiel 3:12, 14, 24; 11:5, 24; 37:14; 39:29; Micah 3:8; Zechariah

4:6). Even Gentile nations recognized the supremacy and presence of the Holy Spirit in those of Israel who were utilized by Him (Numbers 24:1-13; Daniel 4:8, 9; 5:11, 14; Isaiah 45:1-7; Jeremiah 1:1-10).

3. THE DAY OF THE LORD — AT PENTECOST?

Significantly, Joel the prophet predicted a day of renewal for all Israel. The nation could look forward to a time when the Holy Spirit would be poured out on all: male and female, young and old. Such a glorious phenomenon would occur on "the day of the Lord." It would be a special time of judgment on the enemies of Israel, a time of God's people returning to Him with fasting, weeping, and rending their hearts, a time of new grain, new wine, new oil, and a time of salvation for all who call upon the name of the Lord (Joel 2).

Peter made it clear that day had come at Pentecost (Acts 2:14-16). Thus, he called the devout Jews gathered in Jerusalem to salvation in the name of the Lord Jesus Christ and to be recipients of the outpouring of the gift of the Holy Spirit. To refuse would be a tragic rejection that could only invite the judgment of God envisioned by Joel and reiterated by Peter who warned:

> Be saved from this perverse generation. (Acts 2:40)

Later, the writer of Hebrews echoed the same sharp warnings against resisting the Holy Spirit who had now spoken by the Son, the Lord Jesus Christ (Hebrews 1:1-2; 3; 4). With eagerness, broken, and contrite hearts, 3,000 responded to the call of salvation and the gift of the Holy Spirit (Acts 2:41).

4. THE HAND OF THE LORD

Throughout the ministry of the apostles, the presence of the Holy Spirit in the lives of believers became the evidence of the hand of God operating upon them (Acts 4:31, 33; 6:3, 8-10; 7:54-56; 8; 9:17-18; 10:44-48; 11:21-24; 13:1-3; 19:1-7; Romans 8; 1 Corinthians 3:16; 6:19; 12; Galatians 5:16-26; Ephesians 4; Revelation 22:17). It is essential, therefore, that we recognize the person, presence, and the power of the Holy Spirit in our lives as disciples of Christ and His apostles. He regenerates, illuminates, baptizes, empowers, indwells, and equips the believer with spiritual gifts for acts of service. Let us study these aspects of the Holy Spirit.

✎ Regenerating Spirit

In the first place, no one can be saved without the regenerating work of the Holy Spirit. Jesus, in no uncertain terms, explained that for one to enter the kingdom of God, one has to be born of "water and of the Spirit." He further explained that there is a difference between the natural birth and the spiritual birth. The latter is essential for anyone to enter the kingdom of God. Such regeneration is mysteriously done by the Holy Spirit (John 3: 8).

It is the Holy Spirit who convicts of sin, righteousness, and of judgment to come in respect of Christ (John 16:8-11). Notice that Peter was filled with the Holy Spirit on the day of Pentecost. Thus, his message convicted (pricked) the hearts of the crowd inspiring them to change their minds regarding Jesus and to submit to Him as their Lord and Christ.

✎   Illuminating Spirit of Truth

The Pentecostal converts were naturally drawn to the Father through the dynamic influence of the Holy Spirit (John 6:44). He is the Spirit of truth who illuminates the carnal mind to the light of the gospel of Jesus Christ. No wonder Jesus described Him as the Helper sent alongside the believer to bring a realization of the truth about Jesus (John 14:16; 15:26, 27; 16:13-14).

Without the Holy Spirit, we are all naturally blind to the truth about God and cannot understand the message of the gospel of Jesus Christ, which appears as foolishness to the carnal mind (2 Corinthians 4:3, 4). However, as a result of the operation of the Spirit of God, the natural mind is illuminated enabling it to comprehend the spiritual mysteries of God's grace (1 Corinthians 2:6-16). Since it is the Holy Spirit who inspired the writers of Scripture, it stands to reason that He is the One who enables the understanding of those very scriptures, which are only spiritually discerned (2 Peter 1:21; 1 Corinthians 2:14).

✎   Baptized by the Spirit

It is the Spirit of God who baptizes the believer into the body of Christ. The apostle Paul in his letter to the Corinthians instructs us:

> For by one Spirit we were all baptized into one body – whether Jews or Greeks, whether slaves or free – and have all been made to drink into one Spirit. (1 Corinthians 12:13)

We have already explored the concept of baptism in the previous study, but recall the notation that water baptism is a sign of the baptism of the Holy Spirit, which is in view here. The unregenerate human nature is renewed in the image of God from all sinful desires and behaviors. This is done by the washing or renewal of the Holy Spirit that is poured out on us generously through Jesus Christ our Lord (Titus 3:3-7).

Notice based on Paul's letter to Titus,

a.   The unregenerate state before salvation

✎   Foolish

✎   Disobedient

- Deceived

- Slaves to lust and sinful pleasures

- Malice

- Envy

- Hatred

b. The grace of God shown in Christ, brings

   - Kindness

   - Love of God our Savior

   - Mercy

   - Salvation

   - Justification

   - Hope of eternal life

   - Heirs

c. The regenerating work of the Holy Spirit

   - Washes

   - Regenerates

   - Renews

The Holy Spirit is presented here in the act of baptism. He is "poured out on us abundantly through Jesus Christ our Savior (v.6) The imagery used here is the same as that in respect of water baptism, which is indicative of the fact that one is a visible representation of the other. As believers are enjoined to the local body by water baptism, they are simultaneously joined to the mystical body of Jesus Christ by the Holy Spirit. The believer is rendered dead to the world and born again by the regeneration of the Spirit. Therefore, the believer is free to be united to Christ (Romans 6:5; 7:1-6).

- Baptized with Power

By receiving the gift of the Holy Spirit believers are immersed and empowered to serve the kingdom of God. No wonder Jesus instructed His disciples not to leave Jerusalem but to remain there until they were endued with power from on high — the power of the Holy Spirit. They needed that exousia power to be effective eyewitnesses of the truth about the Lord Jesus Christ (Acts 1:5, 8). They needed dunamis (dynamite power) to blast away the lies, hypocrisies, and stony-hearted resistance of the Sanhedrin, Pharisees, chief priests, and elders (Matthew 28:11-15; Luke 4:28, 29-36). They needed kratos power to withstand the steely hegemony of Rome. They needed ischus power to overcome their fears to face a temperamental crowd compromised by sin and conflicted by the confluence of political power, religion, and culture that collided in that kairos moment in Jerusalem A.D. 33 on the day of Pentecost.

All the power needed was supplied by the Holy Spirit. He provides that same power to every Christian who confronts similar challenges in every age. The power of the Holy Spirit enabled Peter, the one who denied knowing Jesus, to stand in defense of Jesus and to defend His honor to the crowd and before the Sanhedrin (Acts 2; 4:9-12). Simultaneously, He enabled the other disciples to stand with Peter and face a crowd that could have easily become an angry mob. Jesus had that experience several times and subsequently, it happened with Stephen and Paul (Acts 7; 9:19-25; 13:50; 14:1-7, 19).

Later, they were empowered to perform extraordinary miracles in defiance of the orders of the Jewish leaders to cease and desist preaching in the name of Jesus (Acts 4:18; 5:27-32). Because of the indwelling presence of the Holy Spirit in the apostles and in the church, priests were converted to the faith, and Samaria was won over by the gospel (Acts 6:7, 8). The chief prosecutor of the Sanhedrin, Saul of Tarsus, was converted (Acts 9:17-19) and Gentiles began to accept Jesus as Savior and Lord all over the Greco-Roman world (Acts 9, 10, 11, 13).

- Indwelling Spirit of God

The Holy Spirit is the gift of God's very presence in the life of the believer. The presence of God tabernacled with the people in the wilderness en route to the Promised Land. Likewise, the Spirit of God abides in the lives of believers individually and collectively as they make their spiritual journey to the new Jerusalem (Hebrews 11:13-16; 12:22-29; Revelation 20:1-4). As the Shekinah glory of God's presence rested in the temple, so too, does the Holy Spirit reside in the body temple of the believers filling them with His divine presence (1 Corinthians 6:17-20; 3:16-17; Romans 8:11). Thus, believers are to be filled with the Spirit exhorting each other in psalms, hymns, and spiritual songs as did the sons of Korah (1 Chronicles 6:31-48; 16; 15:17-22; Ephesians 5:19). Jesus, the very presence of the Godhead in person, tabernacled among His people Israel. In like manner, the Holy Spirit is present in the life of each believer (John 1:4).

- He assures of salvation (Romans 8:14-17).
- He assists in prayer, interceding on believers' behalf (Romans 8:26, 27).
- He acts against carnal behavior (Romans 8:5-11).

Therefore, we ought to be fully conscious of His holy presence in us and govern our behaviors accordingly. We should not grieve Him or quench His holy flame because of our irreverent, carnal behaviors that pollute the temples He has washed and prepared for services (1 Corinthians 6:9-11; Ephesians 4:30). Rather, we are to renew our minds and be transformed into the image of Jesus Christ (Romans 12:1-8).

✎   He Gives Gifts to Believers

As discussed in the preceding segment, not only is the Holy Spirit a gift to believers, the Holy Spirit Himself gives gifts (Greek = *charismata*) to each believer He indwells. This special endowment of grace demonstrates the Spirit's presence and operation in the lives of believers so they may be equipped to serve the body of Christ and the world at large.

Beginning with the apostles, the Spirit of Christ gave supernatural abilities to proclaim the gospel of the kingdom of God and His Christ with accompanying signs and wonders according to His will (1 Corinthians 12-14; Romans 12:1-8; Ephesians 4:1-16). Whenever given and exercised, these spiritual abilities are not for self-aggrandizement, but rather for the glory of God (1 Corinthians 14:20-40; 1 Corinthians 13:1-3; Acts 8:9-24).

Consequently, the church is equipped, edified, and empowered to serve Christ fully by the operation of the Holy Spirit in the apostles, prophets, pastors, teachers, and evangelists He selects and through whom He operates (Ephesians 4:9-16).

As a result, the church achieves unity in the faith, in the knowledge of the sons of God, and maturity in the fullness of Christ. It is important to be aware of what gift you have been endowed with so you may be better able to function as a Spirit-filled member of the body of Christ. These gifts will be discussed fully in the next study unit.

STUDENT ACTIVITIES
—PERSONAL REFLECTION—

The significance of the Holy Spirit in your life as a believer in Jesus Christ cannot be overstated. The Holy Spirit is to be understood as fundamentally essential for us to be saved, to be a part of God's family, and to live in accordance with His will. Failure to be conscious of His abiding presence will result in carnal, un-Christian behaviors that will result in God's chastisement and even death (1 Corinthians 5:1-6; 11:27-30; Hebrews 12:5-13). How aware are you of the Spirit's presence in your life? Your body is to be presented to God daily as a living sacrifice, holy and acceptable to Him. "This is your reasonable service." You are no longer to conform to this world but to be transformed by the renewing of your mind (Romans 8:5-17). In this way, you will manifest the gift(s) with which He will endow you to evidence what is that good and perfect will of God (Romans 12:1-4).

MEMORY GEM

In whom also, having believed, you were sealed with the Holy Spirit of promise, who is the guarantee of our inheritance until the redemption of the purchased possession, to the praise of His glory. (Ephesians 1:13b-14)

JOURNALIZE YOUR JOURNEY

Write down the meaningful insights gained and what has impacted you most in this study segment.

Blessed is the man who… in His law he meditates day and night. (Psalm 1:1-2)

FOR FURTHER STUDY (OPTIONAL)

- Meditate on John 14:25, 26; 15:26, 27; 16:7-15
- Read:
  - *Institutes of the Christian Religion* (Book 1), Calvin, John
  - *The Holy Spirit*, Walvoord, John F, (Zondervan)
  - *The Holy Spirit*, Fergusson, Sinclair B. (IVP)
  - *The Holy Spirit in the Old Testament*, Pink, Arthur (Philadelphia, Fortress)
  - *The Holy Spirit in the New Testament*, Sweete, Henry (London, MacMillan)
  - *Christian Theology*, Erikson, Millard, (Baker pp. 845-883)

NOTE: Write down any questions you need clarified. Submit them to your teacher/facilitator in the next class for helpful responses.

PART II

THE CALL TO FELLOWSHIP

The whole body, joined and knit together by what every joint supplies.
(Ephesians 4:16a)

SCRIPTURE FOCUS

From whom the whole body, joined and knitted together by what every joint supplies, according to the effective working by which every part does its share, causes growth of the body for the edifying of itself in love. (Ephesians 4:16)

PROMPTER GUIDE

In this unit of study, you will learn about:

1. **SPIRITUAL GIFTS (GREEK = *CHARISMATA*)**
2. **THE SPIRIT, THE GIVER**
3. **THE GIFTS**
   A. WORD OF WISDOM
   B. WORD OF KNOWLEDGE
   C. FAITH
   D. HEALING
   E. WORKING OF MIRACLES
   F. PROPHECY
   G. DISCERNMENT
   H. TONGUES (LANGUAGES)
   I. INTERPRETATION OF TONGUES
   J. SERVICE
   K. TEACHING
   L. EXHORTATION
   M. GIVING
   N. ADMINISTRATION
   O. MERCY
4. **PURPOSE OF THE GIFTS**
5. **USE OF SPIRITUAL GIFTS TODAY**

PART II ◆ UNIT D

THE GIFTS OF THE HOLY SPIRIT

INTRODUCTION

In a previous study, we examined how new members are assimilated into the body and how they are discipled by those whom the Lord set over His work. We also studied how the disciples fellowshipped as a community of believers committed to each other's welfare and wellbeing. Such cohesiveness was possible because of the concerted efforts of all who contributed.

Some persons such as Barnabas seemed to have an extra special ability to show love and concern over and above the ordinary. Others tried to duplicate his qualities without the sincerity with which he shared his personal possessions; the results were disastrous. Others like Stephen and Phillip were able to perform miracles and to articulate the Word of God powerfully and with clarity. It is clear that several people were given supernatural abilities to do amazing things (Acts 5:12-16; 6:8; 4:35-37; 8:4-8).

Who gave them these abilities and why? Did they have a choice as to what abilities they could have? What was the purpose of these extraordinary, spiritual abilities? Were those dynamic abilities only for the people we read about in the Bible? Do Christians today experience the same charismatic phenomenon? All these questions will be explored in this study segment as we examine the functions of each member of the body then and now.

1. SPIRITUAL GIFTS (GREEK = *CHARISMATA*)

Recall from our prior study that the church is presented as a body and every member is a part of the body. In the physical body, each cell, tissue, organ, tendon, muscle, and bone performs unique individual physical functions. Similarly, each believer is equipped to serve the church in special, individual, spiritual ways for the benefit of all. These special abilities to serve each other are called spiritual gifts (charismata). These are unique endowments that are granted without merit on the part of the recipients by which they can exhibit extraordinary powers. It is essential that all believers be aware of the gifts they have been granted by the Holy Spirit, the giver of the gifts (1 Corinthians 12:1).

2. THE SPIRIT, THE GIVER

There are diverse gifts, but the Holy Spirit is the One who determines and distributes the gifts (1 Corinthians 12:4-11). He is the sole administrator and dispenser of the gifts to the believer. All the spiritual activities, manifestations, and ministries are under the prevue and by the prerogative of the Holy Spirit (1 Corinthians 12: 4-7).

3. THE GIFTS

a. **The Word of Wisdom** — Godly wisdom is evidenced in speech and concepts that convey the requisites for Godly living; it is the ability to give sound counsel that may draw from the divine revelation of the hidden or complex so as to make good decisions that glorify God.

b. **The Word of Knowledge** — Divine insight that allows one to understand the inexplicable. It is an acute ability to think with an extraordinary depth and to offer counsel that expresses profound reasoning.

c. **Faith** — A deep, resolute assurance and confidence in God and His Word as true and sure. An unwavering conviction of the truth of God's existence and of His Lordship over all people, all things, in all places, in all ages, and in eternity. It is the simple but absolute trust in God's Word as communicated through the Scriptures. Thus, the one endowed with faith will act in total expectation of the fulfillment of the Scriptures.

d. **Healing** — The supernatural ability to remedy a malady or to restore soundness to any diseased condition (Matthew 9:1-8; Luke 9:1). Recovery of health may occur by the declaration of the healer or by the application of care (James 5:13-16; John 9:7).

e. **Working of Miracles** — The supernatural exertion of power to produce an unlikely outcome. The supernatural exhibition of signs revealing the operation of God's activity in the natural affairs of humanity.

f. **Prophecy** — From *pro-pheme* (Greek); to speak forth divine truth pertaining to the behavior of people in relation to the scripture, the kingdom of God, and His mandates as articulated by Christ. Consequently, the prophet may admonish, reprove, and comfort; prophet/prophetess may also predict future events and reveal the hidden, especially as it relates to the kingdom of God and the triumphant return of Christ.

g. **Discerning of Spirits** — The inspired ability to judge between godly and ungodly spirits. It is the capacity to distinguish between those spirits that confess to the Lordship of Christ and those that promote its denial.

h. **Various tongues (languages)** — The different distinct languages and dialects spoken by the different people groups throughout the world. While it is normal to speak in one's native tongue/dialects, it is less natural for one to have the ability to speak in a foreign language to which one has not been exposed or educated. God created the language barrier and it is by His Spirit that He gives some the ability to overcome it and to communicate across it (Genesis 11:1, 5-8; Acts 2:4-8). In his epistle to the Corinthians, Paul hints at tongues of angels, which if spoken, would be unknown unless interpreted (1 Corinthians 13:1 cf. 2 Corinthians 12:3-4)

i. **Interpretation of tongues** — Supernatural ability to understand and translate what is said in the different distinct languages and dialects spoken by the different people groups throughout the world and possibly by angels. The interpreter is given the ability to penetrate the language barrier and travel mentally and linguistically between the two.

j. **Service (ministering)** — Those who are willing to follow the commands of others in the proclamation and promotion of the gospel; the charitable acts of those who render Christian affection, especially to the poor and other disadvantaged groups.

k. **Teaching** — The enhanced ability to impart instruction in a clear and precise manner so that those taught are able to grasp difficult/complex concepts. In respect of the Christian church, it is the endowment of the Spirit to instruct disciples in doctrines expounding, explaining, and instilling the mysterious, which is obscure and inaccessible to the natural mind (Acts 11:26; 8:26-35; Mark 1:21; John 7:14; Matthew 7:29; Ephesians 1:8-10; 3:2-5; Colossians 1:25-27; 1 Corinthians 2:1-14).

l. **Exhortation** — A special form of instruction that encourages, comforts, strengthens, and entreats another that may most often be discouraged, and distressed by adversity and misfortune. The exhorter comes alongside the individual to offer consolation.

m. **Giving** — The spiritual motivation to impart something beneficial to someone else from one's own resources; to furnish or supply what is lacking or needed whether it is requested or recognized; to contribute one's care and well being. While giving is a general act, those specially endowed with this grace are distinguished by their extraordinary, unpretentious, selfless generosity. There is an openness of heart and hand.

n. **Administration** — The extraordinary grace to assume and discharge responsibilities diligently and earnestly. This gift enables the establishment of systems, structures, and processes that make for greater efficiency and effectiveness. It facilitates the governance, leading and direction of people and organizations. It allows for those who are qualified to preside over business affairs to set up the foundational framework upon which to build the work.

o. **Mercy** — The exceptional ability to show kindness to the miserable and the afflicted with deep compassion. It may manifest as the assumption of or the identification with the plight of another induced by the Holy Spirit such that one is moved to action to address the pain or problem. It is evidenced by deep compassion for the suffering of others (e.g. Mother Teresa).

N. B. Not included here are other charismatic endowments of the Holy Spirit such as exceptional strength, extraordinary speed, excellent artistry, and other supernatural abilities (Judges 14:5-7; 15; 1 Kings 18:46;1 Samuel 16:14-23; Exodus 31:1-6).

4. PURPOSE OF THE GIFTS

Each gift as described in Scripture is for a specific use. As members of the body of believers, disciples are not to become enamored with their individual gift(s). Such self-absorption causes one to lose sight of the central purpose of the gifts, which are for the good of all.

Additionally, the gifts are not for self-aggrandizement or personal gain, which is tantamount to their misuse. Misuse of gifts can lead to confusion and disorder in the church in the same way that any physical cell that acts out of sync with the overall function of the body causes disease in the physical body. Similarly, any believer acting selfishly creates discord and dysfunction (1 Corinthians 14:26-33).

As Paul explained to the Ephesian believers, the gifts are dispensed so that

1. Each member may supply his/her contribution to the overall body in love

2. There is synergy, unity, effective growth and maturity (Ephesians 4:16)

3. The purposes of God, who has called us, are accomplished

4. God is glorified by redemption through the blood of Jesus to all who believe

5. Jesus Christ will become the preeminent head of all creation

6. The power and glory of God over heaven and earth are demonstrated (Ephesians 1:7, 20-23)

7. Jesus is also the head of the church (Ephesians 4:15).

The effective exercise of the spiritual gifts by each believer as in the book of Acts will lead to the establishment of the kingdom of God in the earth with Christ as its sovereign head (see Luke 9:1-2; 10:8; 17-20 cf. Matthew 12:28).

5. USE OF SPIRITUAL GIFTS TODAY

When Peter preached on the day of Pentecost over 2000 years ago, he announced the outpouring of the Spirit as the sign of the commencement of the last days. Therefore, it stands to reason that we are in the age of the outpouring of the Spirit even more so. Hence, we may conclude that:

- The gifts are as relevant now as they were then

✎ Until Jesus comes, they must function as instituted

✎ The gifts are needed to overcome every obstacle encountered; without the power of the Holy Spirit the church is powerless

✎ Individual believers will live defeated lives

✎ Each believer must walk worthy of his/her calling in the unity of the Spirit

(1 Corinthians 12-14; Romans 12: 4-8; Ephesians 4:7-16; Revelation 2:7, 11, 17, 26; 3:5, 12, 21; 21:1-4)

6. SUMMARY

✎ Each believer is called and chosen to be part of the kingdom of the Lord Jesus Christ

✎ Each believer has been endowed with spiritual gifts through which God may achieve His purpose of salvation to all mankind

✎ Each believer is to exercise the spiritual endowments to the praise and glory of God's name

✎ Each believer becomes a co-laborer with God using the gifts to make disciples of every ethnicity throughout the world

✎ Each believer is to develop and utilize the gift(s) in love

✎ The church will be edified, equipped, and empowered to accomplish the will of God in Christ Jesus (Ephesians 4:7-16)

STUDENT ACTIVITIES
—PERSONAL REFLECTION—

Imagine yourself as a heart. Your task is to pump the life-giving blood to every cell that will die without your effort. All 100 trillion estimated cells need to receive the precious oxygen that comes from the lungs and each needs the nutrients that were digested in the stomach. At the same time, each cell needs to rid itself of the toxins generated by cellular activity. Your task is to expand and contract repeatedly at the necessary rate of demand by a multiplicity of different processes, functions, and systems so that the body may be kept alive. Think about how unselfishly the heart performs its task from conception to cessation.

Take a quiet moment and listen to your heart. Could you be as dedicated without the excuses and selfish motivations that hinder service?

💡 **MEMORY GEM**

But desire earnestly the best gifts. And yet I show to you a more excellent way. Though I speak with the tongues of men and of angels, but have not love, I have become a sounding brass or a clanging cymbal. And though I have the gift of prophecy, and understand all mysteries and all knowledge, and though I have all faith, so that I could remove mountains, but have not love, I am nothing. And though I bestow all my goods to feed the poor, and though I give my body to be burned, but have not love, it profits me nothing. (1 Corinthians 12:31-13:1-3)

JOURNALIZE YOUR JOURNEY

Write down the meaningful insights gained and what has impacted you most in this study segment.

Blessed is the man who… in His law he meditates day and night. (Psalm 1:1-2)

FOR FURTHER STUDY (OPTIONAL)

- *The Holy Spirit*, Walvoord, John F, (Zondervan)
- *The Holy Spirit*, Fergusson, Sinclair B. (IVP)
- *The Holy Spirit in the Old Testament*, Pink, Arthur (Philadelphia, Fortress)
- *The Holy Spirit in the New Testament*, Sweete, Henry (London, MacMillan)

NOTE: Write down any questions you need clarified. Submit them to your teacher/facilitator in the next class for helpful responses.

Exercise 2d.

List the gifts of the Spirit mentioned in the following passages and answer the questions:

Romans 12:6-8; 1 Corinthians 12:4-11; Ephesians 4:11; 1 Peter 4:11.

1. Which gift(s) do you think you have?
2. According to 1 Corinthians 13, how are the gifts to be exercised?
3. According to 1 Corinthians 14:1-5, 22-25, which gift should be pursued above all and why?
4. Why does the apostle Paul describe that gift as such?
5. Which gift is recommended to be "coveted"?
6. Why is the gift of tongues (languages) not better than the gift of prophecy?
7. What is the primary purpose of the gift of languages (1 Corinthians 14:22, 4).
8. Can we pray for specific gifts?
9. What motivation should drive our requests?

(Teachers read: *Christian Theology* – Millard Erickson, pg. 876)

PART III

THE CALL TO STEWARDSHIP

Let each one give as he purposes in his heart. (2 Corinthians 9:7a)

SCRIPTURE FOCUS

Nor was there anyone among them any who lacked; for all who were possessors of lands or houses sold them, and brought the proceeds of the things that were sold, and laid them at the apostles' feet; and they distributed to each as anyone had need. (Acts 4:34, 35)

So let each one give as he purposes in his heart, not grudgingly or of necessity; for God loves a cheerful giver. (2 Corinthians 9:7)

PROMPTER GUIDE

In this unit of study, you will learn about personal responsibility in the local church in respect of:

1. TITHES AND OFFERING
2. WHAT IS TITHING?
3. GIVING IN THE NEW TESTAMENT CHURCH
4. GIVING TIME
5. GIVING TALENTS (PARTICIPATING IN MINISTRY)

PART III ◆ UNIT A

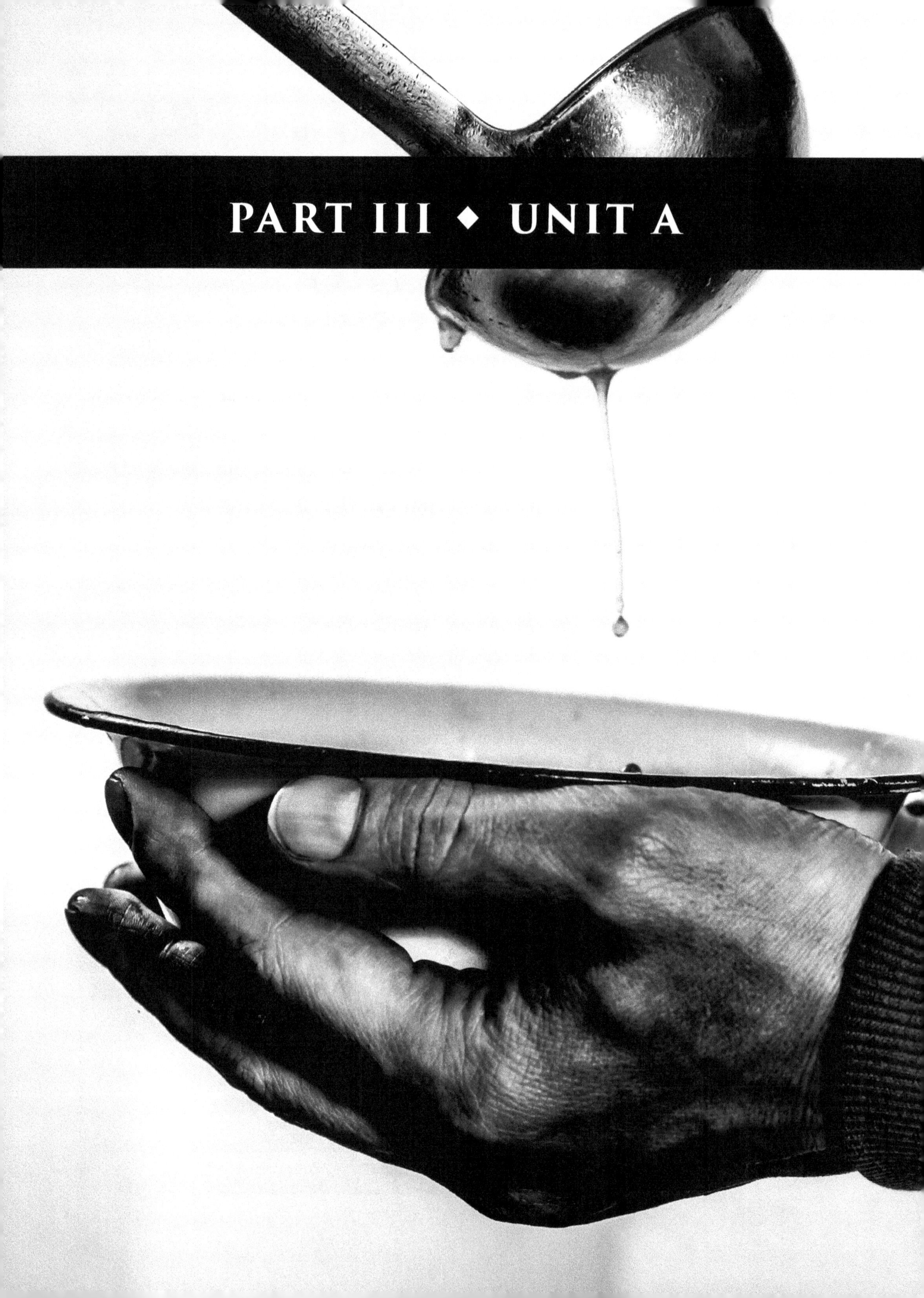

STEWARDSHIP IN THE LOCAL CHURCH

INTRODUCTION

As we continue to learn how to be disciples of Jesus Christ, it is necessary to look at the spiritual contributions we make to the assembly to which we belong. However, we must also consider the tangible, personal contribution of our resources to the church organization. Giving keeps its operations, projects, and programs functioning for the further discipleship of others and ourselves.

Giving monetary gifts for the maintenance and welfare of the church was one of the vital signs of Christian love and brotherhood in the early church as can be seen from the above scriptures. As the church grew in spiritual power and size, many were prompted to share their material wealth so that the needs of other brothers and sisters could be met. This level of self-sacrifice was extraordinary. However, giving was not unusual due to the fact that, to this point, the church was still largely Jewish and the giving of tithes and offerings to the temple for the maintenance of the priest, the Levites, the poor, and even the stranger (non-Israelites) was part and parcel of their socio-religious life (Deuteronomy 26:12; Nehemiah 10:37-39).

It became natural that the apostles, those overseeing the ministry, would be given gifts as acts of worship to benefit others in need much the same way such gifts were given to the priests, Levites, and prophets (Acts 4:35-37 cf. 1 Samuel 9:7, 8).

How did this practice develop as the church incorporated the Gentiles across the Greco-Roman world? What were the practices and precepts of the apostles and church leaders on the matter as they discipled those who joined the body in the emerging new congregations in Samaria, Antioch, Corinth, Ephesus, Galatia, Italy, Spain, and so on?

A more contemporary question we need to consider is: how do we give today in keeping with the faith we have inherited in the churches where we now worship? These are the questions this study segment will discuss to offer some clarity on the issue. While this unit cannot give a full treatment to each of these questions, it is hoped that it will stimulate discussion in the context of the unique church tradition in which the discussion is held and that it will lead to responsible stewardship of our time, talents, and treasure.

1.   TITHES AND OFFERING

The practice of contributing resources to a local church ministry (especially monetary donations), commonly called tithes and offerings, has unfortunately become a controversial one in the modern Christian church. The misuse and abuse of monetary donations by the unscrupulous have largely contributed to this debacle among Christians.

Furthermore, there are those who say that tithing is an Old Testament practice that should not be continued in the New Testament church of Christ. They argue that it is part of the Law; therefore, it is no longer binding on the church. On the other side are those who maintain that it is a valid principle that carried over into the apostolic era. Therefore, it is part and parcel of the obligation of the Christian to the ministry and kingdom of Christ. How can these divergent views be reconciled? Perhaps, what is needed is a primary understanding of some of the key concepts by asking basic questions:

- What is tithing?
- To whom were tithes given/are tithes to be given?
- Why were/are they given?
- When were/are they to be given?
- Where were/are they given?

Hopefully, by answering these fundamental questions, it will be possible to understand the issue better and determine the best course of action for the believer. It is necessary to point out that the issue of tithing cannot be discussed without reference to the complementary act of the giving of offerings as well.

2.   WHAT IS TITHING?

A tithe is a tenth, a tenth part, 10%. 10 is an ancient number for the collective whole. Perhaps, this was conjured from 10 fingers composing the hands and 10 toes composing the feet. The modern metric system is divided into units of tens:

The metric system is decimal, in the sense that all multiples and submultiples of the base units are factors of powers of ten of the unit. Fractions of a unit are not used formally. The practical benefits of a decimal system are such that it has been used to replace other non-decimal systems outside the metric system of measurements; for example currencies[x]

---

x   Wikipedia

In antiquity, a tenth (a tithe) was given as a tribute (tax) to kings, rulers, and authorities. As practiced in the Bible, it preceded the Law of Moses in which regulations for the giving and receiving of tithes and offerings were specified. The practice of giving tithes and offerings is also mentioned in the New Testament era in what could be described as the post Law dispensation.

✎   Tithing in the Patriarchal Period

The first mention of tithing is in Genesis 14:20 where the Patriarch Abraham paid tithes to Melchizedek. This primary reference is pivotal in understanding the entire concept of tithing and giving:

Observations

a.   Abram and Melchizedek   Genesis 14:18, 19

Abraham paid the tithes to Melchizedek. Melchizedek was the priest of the Most High God, king of Salem (Jerusalem), king of peace, king of righteousness (Melchizedek). As such, his priesthood predated the Aaronic order, which was given the charge to receive and distribute tithes and offerings from the people of Israel. In turn, Melchizedek blessed Abraham who paid him the tithe of the spoils he had captured. Abraham tithed out of reverential respect for Melchizedek, not out of any obligation, as say, a tax or tribute. Abraham did so as an act of worship, and He accepted the blessings of Melchizedek in return. In contrast, Abraham refused the offer of Bera king of Sodom to keep portions of the spoils. His perspective of wealth was rooted in God's provision, not worldly possessions.

b.   Jacob   Genesis 28:22

The LORD revealed Himself as the LORD God of Abraham and the God of Isaac to Jacob in a dream. The LORD promised him the land he was sleeping on, that his descendants would be innumerable, He would be with him, He would keep him, He would bring him back to that very land, and He would not leave him until all he was promised happened. In response, Jacob vowed that if the Lord be with him, keep him, feed and clothe him, and return him to his father's house in peace then:

✎   The LORD would be His God

✎   The memorial stone he anointed and erected would be God's house

✎   Of all that God gave, he would give back a tenth to the LORD

✎   Tithing Under the Mosaic Law

Under the Mosaic Law, the tithes were for the maintenance and upkeep of the Levites. The Levites of the tribe of Levi were separated by the LORD to be priests to the rest of the nation of Israel. As a result, they were not given tribal land allotments but small homesteads and cities. Because theirs was an agrarian society, the lack of land allotments would leave the Levites deprived of the means of food cultivation and production to feed themselves and their families. Thus, enshrined in the Law were requirements to offer tithes and offerings to maintain the Levites (Leviticus 27:30-34; Numbers 18). Significantly, the disadvantaged groups: the stranger, the fatherless, and widows were also to be recipients of tithes that were to be made available for their free usage (Deuteronomy 14:22-29; 18:1-8).

Several Bible scholars offer insights into the system of tithing as practiced under the Law. Two of their perspectives help us to appreciate its divine intent and its human benefit:

1.   According to Dennis Writ-Lind, tithing had primary and secondary benefits in the Israelite community and "refers to justice, mercy, and faithfulness." Justice to the Levite, mercy to the poor, and faithfulness to God (cf. Mt 23:33)[xi]

2.   J.B. Payne in *Theology of the Old Testament* describes tithing in two ways:

    a. Godward — He expresses that it was not onerous but a joyful act of worship to the Lord (Deuteronomy 12:12, 28 cf. 1 Corinthians 9:7). He also sees it as a display of submission and dependence (2 Chronicles 31:1-5).

    b. Manward — It maintained community life and fostered the inter-relatedness of the people of God. It allowed for the Levites (deprived, disadvantaged) to be ministered to by the people whose labors and produce were given in tithes to them[xii]. The third-year tithe provided for the poor (especially orphans and widows-defenseless) "the proverbial subjects of neglect...a major step towards a healthy society."[xiii]

✎   Tithing and Giving in the Post Law New Testament Period

Tithing was still in place during the ministry of Christ. Matthew 23:23 notes His observation of the tithing of the Pharisees and scribes which, as Writ-Lind shows, was done devoid of its true intent. Thus, it came under the condemnation of the Lord. It is similarly mentioned in His parable on the prayer of the Pharisee and the Publican (Luke 18:12).

However, the writer of Hebrews goes further and uses the payment of tithes to demonstrate the superiority of the priesthood of Jesus Christ to that of the Aaronic priesthood. He explains that since Aaron paid tithes to Melchizedek in Abraham then Christ is the superior priest because His priesthood is not after the order of Aaron but after the order of Melchizedek. Here, Christ by extension is figuratively portrayed as receiving tithes from Aaron (the lesser to the greater). While Jesus did not actually receive tithes, the writer has no problem associating the receipt of tithes with Him as honorable and indicative of His office as priest.

---

xi   Theology of the Older Testament, pg. 434
xii   Ibid
xiii   Nepho Gerson Laoly, The Tithe (Web Posting, May 8th, 2012)

3. GIVING IN THE NEW TESTAMENT CHURCH

Beyond tithes per se, Jesus was apparently open to receiving the offerings of those who showed Him generosity and kindness. He received monetary gifts from women for His ministry (Luke 8:1-4; John 12:5, 6). He also authorized His apostles to receive gifts when they went forth ministering as He dispatched them (Luke 10:7; Matthew 10:42). Therefore, it was natural for the apostles to receive the gifts of the church (Acts 2:45; 4:32-37; 6:1-2).

Subsequently, as the gospel spread into the Greco-Roman world, monetary aid was collected for one cause or another. Also, members were expected to share their possessions with each other in structured and organized ways as well as on an individual basis motivated by love. For example, Paul spoke to the Corinthians about the collection (1 Corinthians 16:1) and again, of the need, attitude, and Christian philosophy regarding such giving (2 Corinthians 8). In the first instance, the collection was for the saints, and it was ordered to be done on the first day of the week by the church at Corinth and the churches throughout Galatia (1 Corinthians 16:1, 2).

Here, the specific amount to be given was a departure from the required legal tithe of the Jewish economy. The amount given was to be in proportion to one's ability as God had prospered each individually. In the secondary reference, Paul's encouragement to the Corinthians to give provides much insight into the concept of giving in the New Testament churches he established. A cursory examination of the principal words used in the text is instructive.

- Liberality
- Ministry to the saints
- Grace
- Giving of self
- Love
- The example of Christ
- Equality
- Abundance
- Honesty
- Diligence

Observations

I. All of these words used in the texts cited help to illustrate the concept of giving as the church expanded and the needs grew and diversified. Giving was to be of free will and to be a ministry (service) to others. It was to be seen as a grace, a special spiritual endowment of the Spirit, which enables generosity to be shown. That same grace permits selflessness and expression of love that gives of one's abundance to restore equality among the body in honesty and diligence.

II. This charity draws on the example of Christ. He divested Himself of all His heavenly riches to enrich us who, as a result, are blessed with every spiritual blessing (Ephesians 1:1-7). Whereas the traditional tithe is a tenth, Christ gave His all (100%). Hence, giving in the New Testament is not limited to a tenth but unlimited by love. The giving was to meet the needs of the brethren and was to be done cheerfully.

III. Significantly, the giver was not meeting a physical need only, but maintaining the witness of the gospel by supporting the Church, particularly at Jerusalem where the apostles were headquartered (Acts 11:28-30; 15:1-4).

4. GIVING TIME

Giving to the local church must not only be seen in financial terms. Most churches can only function with the voluntary help of many who give of their valuable time. Many churches have elaborate and extensive programs that cater to youth: camps, VBS, mentoring, sports, and after-school activities. Others have television and cable broadcasts reaching many via satellite and the internet. Then, there are missions (local and overseas), evangelism, and community outreach programs offering food, clothing, and shelter to the disadvantaged and the poor. Counseling individuals, couples, and families are also faith-based programs that can be found in the portfolios of many churches.

All these ministries are dependent on and require fund-raising, administrating, managing, and staffing by people who willingly give themselves in service to help others. These individuals spend long hours even after their day jobs and at the expense of their other interests and obligations to volunteer their services. Spending time in the service of Christ is an invaluable gift that results in saving souls and Christian enrichment (Acts 11:22-26; 14:3, 26-28).

5. GIVING TALENTS (PARTICIPATING IN MINISTRY)

Giving time alone is not all that is required. Merely attending a church program is not enough. Sitting in pews and spectating are not the most productive activities. Thus, disciples see the need also to give the church their talents.

Most ministries are staffed by people who have excellent skills and competencies. They have talents that can be used to earn significant incomes in the secular world; however, they choose to offer them to the cause of the kingdom gratis. For example, the multi-media ministries of most churches have personnel who are equally competent to their counterparts in the secular media houses. Nevertheless, they prefer to utilize their lucrative skills for the cause of Christ.

A case in point is the fact that many secular artists will pale in comparison to the vocal and musical abilities of those who minister in the hallowed halls of the church far and away from the spotlights and stages of the world. Yet, these gifted musicians are pleased to overlook the lure of Tinseltown and Broadway for the sheer joy of glorifying God in their assemblies.

As a matter of fact, many accomplished secular artists developed their talents in churches or borrowed their genres of music from them. In other areas, accountants, human resource personnel, administrators, teachers, lawyers, financial advisors, builders, and countless other professionals can all be found busily engaged in the service of Christ. The scriptures are filled with examples of such persons who enriched the church with their skills. Many of them recognized they were equipped by God to so minister to His people (1 Chronicles 16; 25; Exodus 35:30-36).

What natural gift(s) and competencies do you have that may be used to advance the work of the church? What needs have you identified in the local assembly or global church body that you would like to see met? What spiritual gifts do you have or desire to have that could build up others and contribute to the development of the kingdom of God? What irks or irritates you when you see it done poorly or not at all in the church?

STUDENT ACTIVITIES
—PERSONAL REFLECTION—

- How were you evangelized by the church?

- How well was its message delivered to you?

- Were you well received by the brethren when you made the decision to follow Christ?

- What is your perception of the discipleship program, which is designed to help you grow?

- What weaknesses and strengths do you see that may be improved?

- What threats exist that could limit growth and progress?

- Do you see opportunities that could be capitalized on?

All these questions may be used to provoke you to become an active, contributing member of the body of Christ exactly as the Spirit of God intended. Remember you are a steward of the gifts, talents, and resources with which you have been blessed so you may be a blessing to others.

MEMORY GEM

Every good gift and every perfect gift is from above, and comes down from the Father of lights, with whom there is no variation or shadow of turning. (James 1:17)

JOURNALIZE YOUR JOURNEY

Write down the meaningful insights gained and what has impacted you most in this study segment.

Blessed is the man who … in His law he meditates day and night. (Psalm 1:1-2)

FOR FURTHER STUDY (OPTIONAL)

- *Giving and Tithing*, Burkett, Larry (Moody Publishers, 1998)
- *Beyond the Collection Plate*, Durral, Michael (Abingdon Press)
- *Did the Apostle Paul Teach Tithing to the Church?* Kithcart, Jonathan (Winepress Publishing, 2001)
- *The Cycle of Victorious Giving: Your Time, Your Talent, Your Treasure*, Stan and Linda Toler (Beacon Hill Press)

Exercise 3a.

Read the story of the Talents (Matthew 25:14-39) and answer the following questions:

1. What was the perception of the businessman who entrusted his servants with his assets?
2. Why do you suppose different people got different amounts?
3. What do you think the servants who received five and two talents respectively did to double their investments?
4. What was wrong with the actions of the servant who received one talent?
5. How did the master respond to the servants who were industrious as opposed to the one who was indolent?
6. What is your perception of the servant who buried his talent?
7. To which servant's attitude do you seem more closely aligned?

Exercise 3a.2.

Review the following text and write down what you think each is saying about the use of time and abilities:

a.   Ephesians 5:15, 16

b.   1 Corinthians 10:31

c.   Romans 6:13

d.   Romans 12:1-11

PART III

THE CALL TO STEWARDSHIP

Let each one give according as he purposes in his heart.
(2 Corinthians 9:7a)

SCRIPTURE FOCUS

Abide in Me, and I in you. As the branch cannot bear fruit of itself, unless it abides in the vine, neither can you, unless you abide in Me. I am the vine, you are the branches. He who abides in Me, and I in him, bears much fruit; for without Me you can do nothing. (John 15:4, 5)

PROMPTER GUIDE

In this unit of study, you will learn about personal responsibility in the local church.

1. PRINCIPLES TO LIVE BY

A. QUIET TIME WITH GOD

B. TELL SOMEONE WHAT THE LORD HAS DONE FOR YOU

PART III ◆ UNIT B

RELATIONSHIP WITH GOD

INTRODUCTION

Ultimately, Christian Discipleship is a personal decision to follow Christ. To be a student of Christ requires a commitment to continue following Him faithfully by one's own endeavor. 3,000 may have joined the church in total on the day of Pentecost, but each one of those converts had to devote him/herself to the process of discipleship on his/her own. It is the responsibility of each disciple to take up his/her cross daily and follow the Lord (Matthew 10:38; 16:24; Luke 14:27).

As discussed in other units of study, each person has to receive and believe the gospel message individually, and each must confess Christ as Lord for him/herself. Each must also recognize him/herself as a part of the body of Christ and exercise the unique gift(s) bestowed by the Holy Spirit as a vital part of that body.

Most importantly, each believer is responsible for maintaining his/her growth and maturation in pursuit of Christ. Accordingly, it is essential for all disciples to practice spiritual disciplines to grow in the faith. In a physical sense, the same way a daily healthy regimen has to be maintained for a child so that it grows healthy and strong, so too, must a spiritual newborn in Christ maintain a daily spiritual regimen. Below is a tried method of devotional practice reproduced here for your benefit called "Principles to Live By - A Daily Spiritual Regimen." This spiritual discipline will promote and sustain good Christian living. Let us review it and hopefully adopt it for long-term use.

1. PRINCIPLES TO LIVE BY – A DAILY SPIRITUAL REGIMEN

A. Quiet Time with God

A key component of personal discipleship is that of establishing a quiet time with the heavenly Father. In other words, each believer needs to set aside a time for prayer, meditation, Bible study, and solitude in the presence of the Lord one–on–one. Setting up a time to meet God may sound strange. After all, He is not an ordinary person we can contact and put on our calendars, PDA's etc. He is the Lord God Most High.

Nevertheless, while the LORD God is transcendent, He is also the imminent Father; He is everywhere (Psalm 139:1-7). Jesus taught us to pray to Him as our Father. Therefore, if we set aside a time for ourselves to pray to and commune with Him, we will find that He will likewise commune with us (John 14:23; Acts 17:27; Jeremiah 29:13; Revelation 3:20). The preparation is on our part, not the Lord's so we need to pay attention to meeting Him. Here is a simple but effective way to meet with the LORD in quiet time.

- Find a quiet place with minimum disturbance to meet with the Father

A meeting place with God does not have to be exotic or elaborate in terms of décor. The more natural and simple it is, the better. It helps you focus more on why you are there, rather than on religious symbols, artifacts, or furnishings, etc. Some dedicate a room as a prayer room and only use it as such. However, a particular area of a room, a chair in a corner, an attic, a basement, patio, a park bench, an empty church sanctuary during the day or the bathroom are all areas that can be reserved for quiet times. The key is to find a place away from everyone else and anything else that would interrupt you during your quiet time with the Father. Make sure that you minimize disturbances:

- Turn on voicemail on phones/cell phones or turn them off
- Turn off televisions, radios, electronic games/gadgets, etc.
- Tell family and friends not to disturb you except for an emergency during that time
- Have your Bible, notebook/journal, pen with you

- Decide on a time when you will meet consistently

While you may meet with the Father anytime and anywhere, it is good to have a set time to meet Him for your time alone. When it is left to chance, too many competing activities crowd out our time with the Lord. Many have found the early morning hours to be ideal. The advantages of the early morning meeting are:

- The significance of rising early to meet the Lord in prayer (Psalm 63)
- Starting the day with the Lord first
- The quietness of the morning
- The precedent set in Scripture (Genesis 19:2, 27; Exodus 24:4; Psalm 57:8; 63:1; Isaiah 26:9; Jeremiah 7:13; John 8:2)
- Before the business of the day sets in
- To gain spiritual direction and guidance at the onset of each day

Similar benefits may be experienced at other times of the day/night. Some stay-at-home parents find that the best quiet times are when everyone in the household has left for work/

school. The house is quiet and they are alone after the morning rush. Others are more nocturnal and find the late hours of the night better times to reflect on the day past and prepare for the day ahead. Whichever time is more suitable ought to be decided on and used.

- Begin with a short simple prayer of adoration and thanksgiving

Begin by thanking the Lord for the gift of a new day of life and for His protection and preservation through the past night (trying not to slip into a "laundry list" of needs prayer unless you are burdened or led by the Spirit to intercede on some matter). Scriptures such as Lamentations 3:23; Psalm 57: 7, 8; 63:1-3, can be drawn on to focus the mind on meeting God in the morning and adoring Him for the privilege of being able to do so. The fact that He saved us through His own Son and desires a relationship with us is more than enough reason to give praises to God on rising. Here are some other examples:

Open my eyes, that I may see wondrous things from your law. (Psalm 119:18)

Search me, O God, and know my heart; try me, and know my anxieties. (Psalm 139:23)

Your word is a lamp to my feet and a light to my path. (Psalm 119:105)

Blessed are You, O Lord! Teach me Your statutes. (Psalm 119:12)

The Psalms, especially 119, are replete with excellent introductory prayers you may use to commence your quiet time.

- Study the Gospel of St. John

Especially for new believers, John's Gospel proves to be an excellent exposé on the life of Jesus Christ. The apostle John, the writer, is very clear about the reason he wrote the account of Jesus' life. He wanted those who read it to believe that Jesus is the Christ, the Son of God, and that believing you may have life in His name. (John 20:31)

In John's account of the life and ministry of Jesus, we meet the divine Savior, the Word (Greek = *logos*). He is the One who is the consummate wisdom and power in union with God, the maker of all creation, the ruler of the universe, and the cause of all that exists in the world both physical and eternal. In Greek thought, John presents Jesus as the total explanation of all that may be understood of God, mankind, and all creation. He is the reason and cause of all things. He is the Word made flesh that dwells among us whose glory is that of God the Father full of grace and truth (John 1:1-3, 14, 18).

Moreover, in his Gospel narrative, John portrays a very human Jesus engaging the ordinary and the outcast, the noble and the notable. He does so with deep compassion and compelling concern. Nowhere in the other gospel accounts can we read more of Jesus' one-on-one dialogues with people and nor His self-declarations that give deep insight into His self-concept as in John's account. John gives us an intimate portrait of our Lord from the one called the beloved disciple who reclined on His bosom in devotion. Since the disciple is a follower of Jesus then a close-up view of the LORD is best had in the book of John (John 21:20; 13:23).

Read the book of John in small portions. Trying to read an entire chapter all at once may be unnecessary. The point is to study Jesus, not complete the readings about Him. It is best to study small units of the scriptures at a time indicated by where the natural breaks in the narrative occur.

- Be conscious of the Holy Spirit as you read and study

Recall from the study on the Holy Spirit that He is the One who convicts and convinces us of the truth of the Word of God and draws us to the Father. His work of regeneration also involves the renewing of the mind by helping us to understand spiritual truths, which cannot be discerned by mere human intellect (1 Corinthians 2:14-16). God has concealed some deep truths regarding Himself and His work of salvation in His Word.

The spiritual illuminating power of the Holy Spirit opens our eyes to those mysteries much the same way Jesus did when He taught His disciples (Luke 8:9 -10; Matthew 13:51, 52; Luke 10:21-24). In the same way, Jesus has sent the Holy Spirit to enable our understanding (John 15:26-27).

Therefore, be aware of His indwelling presence and cultivate your spiritual ears to listen to His gentle unveiling of truth in your heart. He will lead you into all truth, which convicts the world of sin, righteousness, and judgment to come.

- Journalize thoughts, insights, questions, and doubts encountered

As you read the book of John, allow the scriptures to engage your intellect reflecting deeply on what is read:

- Write down any truths learned and any thoughts that emerge freely
- Jot down questions or concerns for further study or research
- Note any scriptures that stick out and commit them to memory
- Apply any principles learned in your daily living. For example, the story of the blind man in John 9 may provoke these questions:
  - Am I blind as well?
  - Am I unwilling to see the truth that the Lord presents plainly before me?
  - What resistance do I show to deny Christ in my life or the life of others?
  - Am I ashamed to testify about the Lord?
  - Do I judge people's misfortunes by appearances and according to cultural norms or based on the Word of God?

🖊 Why did the disciples think the man had sinned and, therefore, was responsible for his blindness when he was blind from birth? And so on.

Journalizing enables one to map growth and development. Documenting one's insights and experiences is the compiling of literary photographs, which may be reflected on at later times. By so doing, the journal will show growth in understanding over time as questions are answered. It will mark the points in life where faith may have deepened, when difficulties were weathered, and how triumphs were achieved.

Journalizing will etch footprints that may be retraced over a period of time with good benefits. Often, insights that were written at one time will reveal their profound nature at another. You will be amazed at the very rich thoughts you had as your mind was illumined by the Holy Spirit in your times of study and meditation.

At other times of reflection, you will marvel at how naïve you may have been and how many of the questions that stumped you initially can now be well answered. The Gospels, for example, to a limited extent, document the growth in the lives of the apostles of Jesus as they developed from mere fishermen, primarily, to bold competent witnesses able to articulate the scriptures to the amazement of the Sanhedrin (Act 4:13). A personal journal can serve a similar purpose.

🖊 Pray about what you've read about

Having written down thoughts, questions, and insights, spend time praying about what was read and studied. It is quite easy to offload our "laundry list" of requests to the Lord telling Him everything we want, wish, and desire. However, we need to cultivate a more disciplined way to communicate with God first. Since we are His disciples, His will ought to be our highest priority. His Word, the Bible, reveals His will to us and for us. It contains God's burden for His people and His desire for those who are yet to become His people.

Thus, when we read His Word, we want to be careful to see whether what we have read communicates His will for our present circumstances. For example, if we go back to John 9, our prayer could be asking the Lord to open our eyes to see what He wants us to see. It may be to give us the boldness to be unashamed of our past blindness because now that we have met Jesus, our spiritual eyes have been opened. It may be to pray for parents bound by societal pressure or for religious leaders unwilling to accept that God works in unusual ways, which challenge our traditions and beliefs. All these may be drawn from the text read.

Praying this way focuses our attention on the issues that matter to the Lord. It redirects us from our selfish desires to the matters of the kingdom, which are concerned with the life and death of the people of the world including those closest to us. The more minute issues of our lives are thus brought into perspective. The scriptures warn us against vain prayers that are so selfishly motivated that God does not answer them (James 4:3). Once we have ministered to the Lord, we are free to express all our cares to Him. He is interested in all our concerns. We are admonished:

Casting all our care upon Him, for He cares for you. (1 Peter 5:7)

For we do not have a High Priest who cannot sympathize with our weaknesses, but was in all points tempted as we are, yet without sin. Let us therefore come boldly to the throne of grace, that we may obtain mercy and find grace to help in time of need. (Hebrews 4:15, 16)

For your Father knows the things you have need of before you ask Him ... therefore ... do not worry. (Matthew 6:8, 25-34)

Further, the Holy Spirit, Himself, intercedes on our behalf with groanings that are too deep for words so that the will of the Father is realized in our lives (Romans 8:26, 27). He works all things together for our good because we love Him and He loves us. Hence, in this relationship, we need not panic that our cares will be unaddressed. Rather, we need only trust and direct our prayers on the behalf of the needs of the kingdom so that His will may be done on earth as it is in heaven. (Matthew 6:9-13).

It is amazing how when we discipline ourselves to pray according to the will of God as expressed in His Word that it shapes our prayers and the focus of our lives as well. We become better witnesses for the kingdom of God when we pray as directed by the Word of God as we read daily and consistently in a systematic way.

✎   Listen to God's voice

Spending quiet time with the Lord is also about listening in silence. After you pray out loud, spend some time quietly listening to the Spirit of the Lord speaking to you. As was stated earlier, you need to be aware that God talks to us by His Holy Spirit who is our counselor and guide. By listening in anticipation, we cultivate an ear to hear the Lord speak to us. Don't be perturbed at the sound of the noises about you or within you that fill those moments. In time, they will become background noises to the voice of your LORD.

Don't be distracted by your thoughts. In time, they too, will become instruments of God's communication to you. Often, in such moments, the Lord may impress others on your heart/mind that you may need to speak to and share with them what He has spoken to you. Pray for the opportunity to do so.

B. Tell Someone Else What The Lord Has Done for You

As we grow in grace and in the knowledge of our Lord and Savior Jesus Christ, it is important that we share our faith with others in a natural and forthright manner. As an outgrowth of our time with the Lord, you will find that there is a growing desire to invite others to experience that same joy you find in the presence of the Lord. You need not think that you have to become an evangelist or a Bible scholar to share your Christian faith. On the contrary, you need only tell others what happened to you since you became a disciple of Jesus Christ.

A genuine Christian experience is impactful and meaningful to others. Actual personal testimony is often far more effective than a theological discourse of the Bible. Biblical treatises are expressions of objective truth. However, your personal testimony is a subjective but specific experience of objective truth in your life that cannot be refuted.

Consider the impact of the Samaritan woman who ran throughout the town inviting people and calling out: "Come see a Man who told me all things that I ever did. Could this be the Christ?" (John 4:29). Recall the blind man who told people what Jesus did to open his eyes (John 9:11, 15, 17, 30-33). In each case, a simple relating of the story of what the Lord had done was enough to change entire towns and bring their inhabitants to Jesus. You can do the same. Your story is valuable and vital. Tell it!

STUDENT ACTIVITIES
—PERSONAL REFLECTION—

The entire body of Christ increases and is edified as each part functions and supplies its yield to the corporate body of the church. The effectual working of the Holy Spirit in each disciple causes the entire body to grow up in love complementing its head, even Christ. Your personal growth or lack of growth determines the health of the entire Christian body. Think about how your individual actions affect the assembly where you worship.

MEMORY GEM

As newborn babes, desire the pure milk of the word, that you may grow thereby, if indeed you have tasted that the Lord is gracious. (1 Peter 2:2, 3)

JOURNALIZE YOUR JOURNEY

Write down the meaningful insights you gained and what has impacted you most in this study segment.

Blessed is the man who…in His law he meditates day and night. (Psalm 1:1-2)

FURTHER STUDY (OPTIONAL)

- Read the story of Chuck Colson in his book *Born Again*
- Read *Betrayed*, Stan Telchin, Tuscan, 2007
- Consider writing your story of conversion. It may become a powerful testimony of the grace of God that encourages others to believe as well.

Exercise 3b.

Review the following text and try to gain a sense of the writers' devotional experiences in each case:

- Genesis 24:62, 63
- Joshua 1:1-8
- Psalm 1
- Psalm 63:1-6

- Psalm 77:12
- Psalm 119:23, 48, 78
- Psalm 143:5
- 1 Timothy 4:1-15

Exercise 3b.2.

Read the story of the demoniac of Gadara (Mark 5:1-20) and discuss the following:

1. What was wrong with the man Jesus met?

2. What does it mean to be demon possessed?

3. What did Jesus do to deliver him?

4. What were the results in the man's life?

5. How did the townspeople react to the dramatic exorcism?

6. What was the man's desire?

7. What did Jesus tell him to do instead?

8. What did he do?

9. What was the effect?

10. How do you think his story affected the view some first held about Jesus?

PART III

THE CALL TO STEWARDSHIP

*Separate to Me Barnabas and Saul for the work
to which I have called them. (Acts 13:2b)*

SCRIPTURE FOCUS

As they ministered unto the Lord and
fasted, the Holy Spirit said, "Now
separate to Me Barnabas and Saul for
the work to which I have called them."
Then, having fasted and prayed, and
laid hands on them, they sent them
away. (Acts 13:2, 3)

PROMPTER GUIDE

In this unit of study, you will learn about personal
responsibility in the local church.

1. PERSONAL EVANGELISM
2. CORPORATE EVANGELISM
3. MISSIONS

PART III ◆ UNIT C

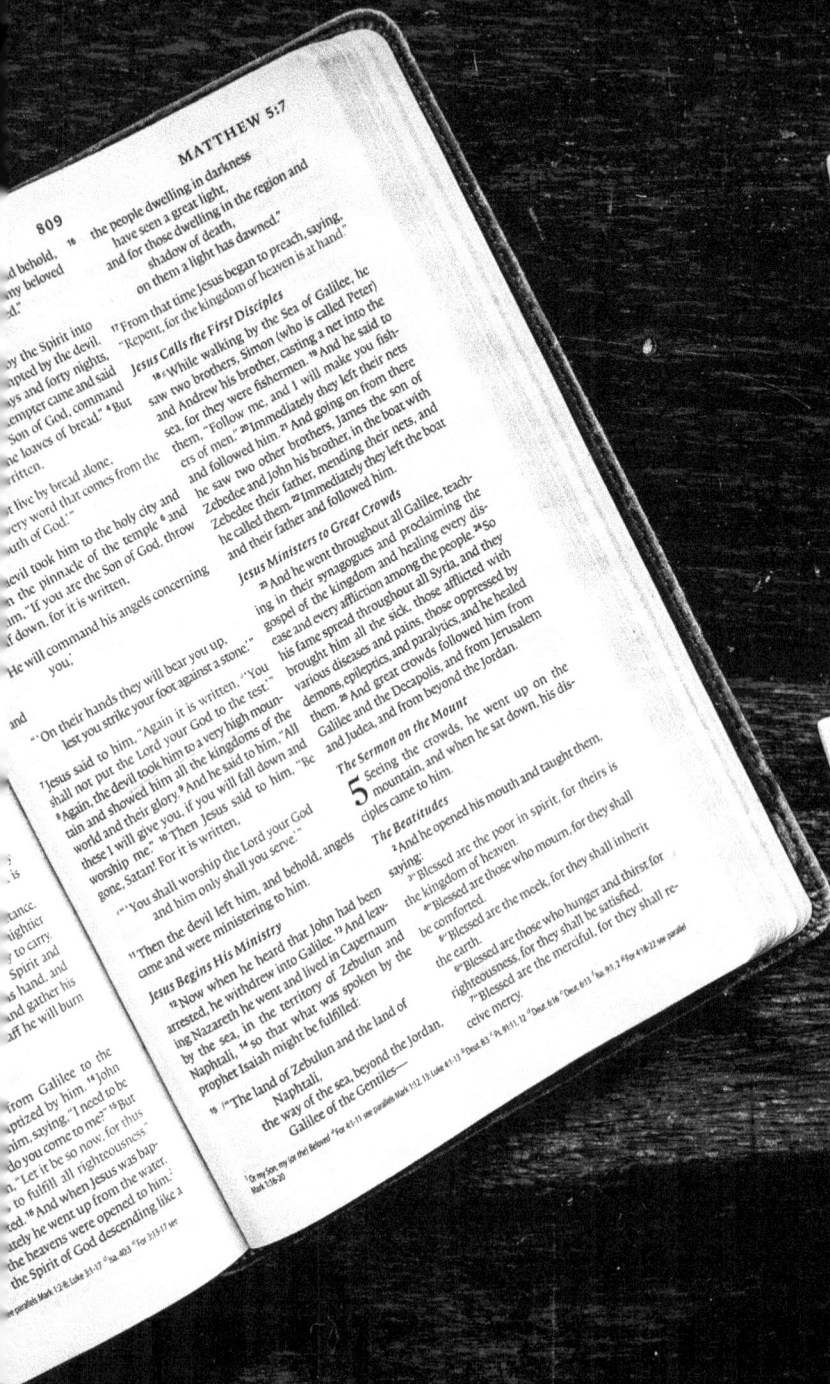

SALT AND LIGHT

RELATIONSHIP WITH THE WORLD

INTRODUCTION

By now, it should be evident that discipleship is a dynamic, ongoing activity in the life of the believer in Jesus Christ. It does not end once a believer has been schooled in the doctrines of the faith and has begun to observe them in his/her individual life. Rather, it continues in such a way that each discipled believer disciples others they encounter in their daily lives. This activity is called evangelizing — the act of sharing the good news of the gospel with the world. This is a simple definition, which may be sufficient for our purposes here but Dr. Robert Fern offers a more comprehensive definition from Canon Bryan Green in his book, *The Power of Cooperative Evangelism (EMIS)*:

> *Evangelism is the proclaiming of Christ Jesus in the power of the Holy Spirit that men should come to put their trust in God through Him, accepting Him as Saviour and Him as Lord of their personal life and in the corporate fellowship of the church*[xiv].

Let us study this soul-winning activity so we may practice it as disciples of Jesus Christ who commissioned His disciples to do so.

> All authority has been given to Me in heaven and on earth. Go therefore and make disciples of all the nations, baptizing them in the name of the Father and of the Son and of the Holy Spirit, teaching them to observe all things that I have commanded you... Amen. (Matthew 28:18-20)

Armed with this divine mandate, we must realize that discipling others with the gospel is neither a mere traditional practice of the church nor is it as some critics believe, the bigoted attempt to impose our religious beliefs on others. Rather, it is the primary imperative from the Lord Jesus Christ Himself.

It is the divine will that the gospel of the kingdom is proclaimed to every living creature of every ethnic group throughout the world. The growth of the kingdom is dependent on

---

xiv   Bryan Green, The Power of Cooperative Evamgelism, (EMIS)

it and the appearance of the kingdom in visible fullness awaits it. It is not the will of the Father that any should perish but all should come to repentance (2 Peter 3:9; Matthew 24:14).

Notice that Jesus' emphasis in His commission stated above is threefold:

1. Making disciples

2. Baptizing those disciples

3. Teaching those disciples to observe all that He commanded

Evangelizing is the Christian disciple's principal responsibility. It is the proclamation of the gospel so that disciples are made, baptized, and taught to observe the Word, the will, and the way of Christ.

Every Christian was evangelized with the gospel. Therefore, in turn, every Christian must evangelize others as the Spirit leads exercising the very gifts with which the Spirit has endowed them. It may be done individually, (personal evangelism) or collectively (corporate evangelism) via formal missionary efforts locally and abroad (missions). Evangelism must consist of both the proclamation and the practice of what is believed and preached. Each of these methods of evangelism is briefly reviewed here in this study, but the full understanding and mastery of each will require specialized study and practice.

In all of them, the goal is two-fold:

a. To commend the saving love of God in Christ Jesus to all who will receive it. (Romans 5:8)

b. To warn of the condemnation of those who refuse to receive God's Son as Savior. (John 3:18,19)

Let us review the methods of evangelism mentioned above.

1. PERSONAL EVANGELISM

The gospel is the story of God. It portrays Him as Savior of lost humanity whom He loves so much in spite of its sinfulness that He sacrificed His beloved Son to save all. Each of us is part of that story because we are members of the human race for whom Christ died and to whom the Father offers His love and salvation.

> For God so loved the world, that he gave his only begotten Son, that whosoever believeth in him should not perish, but have everlasting life. For God sent not his Son into the world to condemn the world; but that the world through him might be saved. (John 3:16, 17 KJV)

While God offers salvation to all, notice that each one must exercise personal faith to receive it individually as you have done. Personal evangelism is centered on this dynamic.

✐   One-on-One

One–on-one evangelism is the two-way interaction of the Christian on the one hand, and the unsaved friends, relatives or strangers on the other as the case may be. It is the personal engagement of a believer with a non-believer(s) sharing the good news of the kingdom of Jesus Christ. The objective is to persuade that non-believer(s) to surrender to the Lordship of Jesus as the will of God prescribes. Here, the emphasis is on an individual in whom the Spirit of God is operative to give the message of salvation to another. Hence, the believer is moved to share the Word of God informally or formally with others to the saving of their souls formally and informally (Acts 8:26-40).

✐   Informal evangelizing

Informal evangelizing takes place in everyday interactions: telling one's testimony to friends in casual conversations, sharing over a cup of tea with a neighbor, talking in the bus, train, or plane with a fellow traveler or even with a perfect stranger in a chance encounter. In other words, informal, personal evangelizing occurs wherever and whenever the opportunity arises to share the message of salvation. This may seem haphazard and unplanned, but each believer must be prepared to be so used by the Lord knowing that His plan is the salvation of all.

✐   Formal evangelizing

Formal evangelizing may occur when an appointment is made to discuss the gospel at a neighbor's kitchen table, over a meal, at the office or some other meeting point. In this case, the parties both expect to be engaged in a discussion about the Bible and what it says regarding one's need for salvation. It may also be part of a small group Bible study at work or at a home where the gospel is presented and hopefully accepted.

Whether formal or informal, the "evangelists" need to trust God to orchestrate the interface. He is the best person by His Holy Spirit to engineer the encounters so that His plan of salvation is mysteriously executed in the lives of people we appear to meet by chance or more often by the providence of God. Therefore, each believer should always be ready to give everyone an answer concerning the hope of salvation within him/herself in season and out of season (1 Peter 3:15; 2 Timothy 4:2). Here are some examples in the scriptures of personal, one-on-one encounters:

✐   John 1:40-42 — Andrew to Simon (brother to brother)

✐   John 1:43-51 — Phillip to Nathaniel (friend to friend)

✐   John 4:5-42 — Jesus to the woman (stranger to stranger)

✎   John 3:1-21 — Jesus to Nicodemus (Savior to the intellectual/religious)

✎   Acts 8:26-40 — Philip to the Ethiopian eunuch (evangelists to the curious)

Notice that in each example cited in the Scriptures above there was a natural sharing of the message of salvation to the person engaged. There were no formal appointments set up to discuss the experience of those who wanted to share except perhaps, in the case of Nicodemus. Nevertheless, there was a passionate, exuberant motivation that prompted the conversations. Also, there was, in some cases, a personal interest on the part of the witness in the other person. For example, Andrew to his brother Simon and Philip to Nathaniel. In the others, God was specifically at work to bring about a grander purpose beyond the individual. What do you think that purpose may have been in the Samaritans and the Ethiopians? Who were they?

2. CORPORATE EVANGELISM

In contrast to personal, individual efforts to share the gospel, corporate evangelism is done collectively by the church body. It may happen in several ways and formats. For example, a local church may hosts a series of evangelistic services where an evangelist is the featured speaker nightly at a church, outdoor meetings or perhaps, a tent as the case may be.

Alternatively, the church may organize a tract (pamphlet) distribution campaign in a neighborhood or a door to door campaign where teams of members participate in spreading the gospel in preplanned events. In corporate evangelism, the initiative comes from the leaders of the church and the membership. The corporate body is mobilized as a result. Billy Graham's Crusades are perhaps the most renown in recent times of corporate evangelism. At these crusades, many churches come together to impact an entire city/country with the direct admonition to repent and believe the gospel.

3. MISSIONS

As the name suggests, "missions" is another form of evangelism. It refers to the sending of a person or a group of persons to accomplish a specific service(s) (Webster). In this case, missions would be concerned with the sending forth of Christian workers to propagate the gospel. The goal is to persuade the people to whom they are sent, to receive the gospel and become disciples of Jesus Christ.

Throughout Scripture, there are numerous instances where God sent forth persons to carry His Word to others or to accomplish His will by doing the task(s) He assigned (Isaiah 6:8, 9). We can say that Noah and his family were given the mission of saving those who would heed his warning by building an ark before the global flood. Abraham was given the mission to go to a new land, Canaan, to start a new nation of people who would live in a peculiar covenant relationship with God. Moses was given the mission of delivering the people of Israel from Egypt and to lead them into the Promised Land. Prophets, priests, and kings who descended from the tribes of Israel were often directed to accomplish various campaigns on the behalf of God and for the salvation of His people.

Of course, the greatest envoy of God was Jesus, His Son (Hebrews 3:1-2). He came to be the Savior of the entire world. According to the will of God, He died a vicarious death for the salvation of all mankind. In turn, Jesus sent forth others He called and trained (disciples) to proclaim the gospel and to establish communities of believers in His name (Matthew 28:18-20; Luke 24:44-48; Mark 16:15-20; John 20:21).

Establishing communities of disciples has continued down through the centuries over the past 2000 years to our day. There were times in history that entire nations were preoccupied with the sending of missionaries to spread the gospel or were transformed by the coming of such missionaries to their lands. The apostles sent forth envoys to Antioch and Antioch to Asia-Minor and Europe. In turn, Europe (particularly England), dispatched Christian missionaries to America, Africa, India, Asia, and the far reaches of the world.

That same missionary effort is now ours to fulfill having been evangelized with the gospel through the obedience and sacrifice of others. These missionaries went where they were sent and to whom they were sent, at times at the cost of their lives. Today, particularly in countries that are hostile to Christianity, many believers continue to be martyred. Yet, there are those who soldier on at the command of the Captain of our salvation who bids them do so (Revelation 2:8-13). These ought to be supported and prayed for as they make supreme sacrifices for the kingdom of God and His Christ our Lord (Hebrews 13:3).

With the advancements in technology, the necessity of having to physically interface with people in foreign lands is significantly reduced. The advent of television, cable networks, the internet, CDs, DVDs, and digital technology has made it possible to spread the gospel without leaving one's country. However, no electronic media will ever replace human-to-human contact that provides face-to-face communication of the gospel in the presence of human need and suffering. Now, perhaps more than ever, the church needs to utilize every means of communication and still go to make disciples of all ethnic groups throughout the world.

As you go, wherever you go in life, spread and share the gospel. Send forth the gospel as an evangelist, a witness among the members of your church, a missionary, and as an example to your household, family members, friends, neighbors, work colleagues, and the world at large. All those whom the Lord draws to Him in response to your testimony must be discipled and integrated into a sincere local church. This must be a church committed to the edifying, equipping, and empowering of believers for their growth and maturation in the Lord Jesus Christ.

STUDENT ACTIVITIES
—PERSONAL REFLECTION—

How can you be an effective witness for Jesus? Wherever you go in life, you can spread, share, and send forth the gospel as an evangelist. Simply being an example to your household, family members, friends, neighbors, work colleagues, and the world at large is a good place to begin. Who in your social network knows that you are a Christian by what you communicate or spend time viewing? Pray to be used by the Lord as His witness or as an evangelist/missionary. Ensure that all those whom the Lord draws to Him in response to your testimony are discipled and integrated into a sincere local church that is committed to the edifying, equipping, and empowering of believers for their growth and maturation in the Lord Jesus Christ.

MEMORY GEM

You therefore, my son, be strong in the grace that is in Christ Jesus. And the things that you have heard from me among many witnesses, commit these to faithful men who will be able to teach others also. (2 Timothy 2:1, 2)

JOURNALIZE YOUR JOURNEY

Write down the meaningful insights you have gained. What has impacted you most in this study segment?

Blessed is the man who … in His law he meditates day and night. (Psalm 1:1-2)

_____

FOR FURTHER STUDY (OPTIONAL)

- Investigate notable, historic missions of the Christian church and seek to discover what made them so, whom God used to affect them, and how.

- Contemplate how you may be used to impact the world with the gospel as was done by those who have gone before us. Consider reading the following in your research:

- *The Great Awakenings*, Dr. David Livingston

- *Welch Revival*, George Lisle (Liele), George Muller

- *The Matyr of the Pongas*, Henry Caswell

Exercise 3c.

The class may be divided into groups to study each scenario above and make observations afterward. A spokesperson from each group may report on their findings to the class.

Review Questions: (Study each encounter)

1. What made each encounter personal?

2. What prompted the conversations?

3. Was any pressure applied to the persons involved?

4. In which cases were the initiatives human and in which were they divine?

5. How were the "evangelists" received by those who shared the good news with them?

6. Which was formal?

7. Which was informal?

Exercise 3c.2.

(Divide the class into groups to review and report on the scriptures given below)

- Disciples are sent out officially by Jesus (Luke 9:1-6; 10)
- Samaria is evangelized (Acts 8:5-25)
- Outreach Antioch (Acts 11:19-30)

Review Questions

1. Where were the disciples directed to go?

2. Whose idea was it for the disciples to go into the villages?

3. What were they to do specifically?

4. What were they told not to do and why?

5. Who empowered them to preach, heal the sick, and cast out demons?

6. What organization was put in place to manage their efforts?

Exercise 3c.3.

Divide the class into groups to discuss the scriptures cited.

How willing are you to serve God in the face of hostility? Here are some examples of missions in the scripture that would inform us to do as the Lord directs through the local and international church bodies to which we belong/serve:

Biblical Missions

1. Isaiah 6

2. Jeremiah 1:1-10

3. Peter and company to Cornelius (Acts 10)

4. Philip to the Ethiopian eunuch (Acts 8:26-40)

5. Paul and Barnabas to Antioch (Acts 11:19-26)

6. Paul and Barnabas to the nations (Acts 13:1-5)

7. Paul and his team to Asia-Minor (Acts 13-52)

8. Timothy to various churches (1 Corinthians 4:17; 2 Corinthians 1:1; Philippians 2:20)

9. Titus to Corinth (2 Corinthians 8:16-24)

It would also be helpful to study historic missions that were undertaken by outstanding men and women of God who carried the gospel to nations abroad.

APPENDIX

1. NEW MEMBERS ORIENTATION

Aim

The purpose of the New Members Orientation is to give new believers/new members excellent starts to their beginnings in Christ. How a person begins is integral to his/her progress and development in all areas of life. Equally, orientation is one of the critical first steps in this program of discipleship. It may determine how well the entire study is undertaken and its lifelong implications. Therefore, aim to make this first step one that will lead each student to spiritual maturity in Christ as he/she is introduced to new life in Christ and being a new member of your local assembly.

Approach

Ephesians 3:1-7; 4:11-16; Colossians 1:19-23; 2 Corinthians 5:17; 6:1; Hebrews 13:20, 21

Reflect deeply on the above scriptures as you prepare for your orientation session. Take note of the following principles derived from those scriptures. As you meditate on them, they will help shape your mind, attitude, and spirit to accomplish your task of discipling others with the following realization:

- The knowledge you share is not commonplace
- You are conveying deep and profound mysteries of the kingdom of God to those He intends to receive them
- You reveal the indwelling Christ — the hope of glory
- Your ministry is that of reconciling the lost to God
- You are only worthy to do so by His grace
- You are specially gifted by God for your tasks
- You are God's ambassador pleading to a lost world that God loves
- Your role allows you to equip and edify the body of Christ
- Your work leads to the maturation of others in the truth of the knowledge of Christ
- Your work prevents susceptibility to false doctrines
- Your ministry fosters the unity of the faith
- Your labor of love is empowered by God's Spirit in you

Perspectives to Consider

a. New Believers

A proper start is extremely important for new converts. New believers tend to judge their Christian experience by their first contact with the assembly. One of the first impressions they will have is you — their teacher and guide. They will perceive you as a representative of what they should become, which is a disciple of Christ; after all, you were selected to teach them.

Therefore, it is not unreasonable for them to make assumptions based on the following:

- The information you give
- The Bible from which you teach
- God
- The Church
- Christianity as you minister to them

In fact, you can represent or misrepresent the Bible, the doctrines you present, the Church, the pastor(s), and most importantly, Jesus Christ your Lord (those who are all relying on you).

With this enormous responsibility in mind, you must be determined to be the best representative you can be. Don't be intimidated, however. Do what you have been trained to do and do it well. Ultimately, you know it is God's Spirit working in you Who will accomplish the work according to the good pleasure of His will (Philippians 2:13). Yield to Him.

b. Believers Joining the Local Church

Orientation is equally critical for believers joining the local assembly for the first time. You should not assume or take anything for granted. Bear in mind that although they may have been members of other assemblies, some may never have been discipled before. It is now our intention and responsibility to ensure they are properly instructed in sound doctrine to produce effective growth in their lives (see 1 Timothy 1; Acts 19:1-7).

Also consider that others in this category may have had good and bad experiences in the assemblies from which they came. Therefore, their preconceived notions may influence their perception of you and the way they relate to you. They, too, need effective fresh starts to re-energize their growth in Christ. You can provide it just as Jesus did (Matthew 5-7).

c. Preparation

Ephesians 3:1-7; 4:11-16; Colossians 1:19-23; 2 Corinthians 5:17; 6:1; Hebrews 13:20, 21

Meditate on the foregoing scriptures to gain a proper perspective before you minister to those God has entrusted you to disciple.

Ahead of time, pray for the class members scheduled to attend that they do not let the Enemy or any other distractions keep them away. Also, pray that they may be receptive to the material they will receive at each session. Pray that they will continue and not draw back (Hebrews 10:38, 39).

Pray with the other teachers and facilitators who are working with you and for the general church congregation. Ask God to inspire them to receive the new disciples well and offer them the nurturing environment they will need to grow in Christ.

Our Prayer for You

> Now may the God of peace who brought up our Lord Jesus from the dead, that great Shepherd of the sheep, through the blood of the everlasting covenant, make you complete in every good work to do His will, working in you what is well pleasing in His sight, through Jesus Christ, to whom be glory forever and ever. Amen. (Hebrews 13:20, 21)

Orientation Session Format

The following is a tested format recommended for your use. Variations may be made for practical necessity and in consultation with the orientation team leader/pastoral leadership. It is not to be changed at the whimsical discretion of facilitators.

Seating

Wherever possible, seat participants in a circle to encourage participation and interaction. A circle allows everyone's face to be seen and fosters better relationships among participants. These dynamics should be encouraged constantly in class.

Sign-in

Have participants sign in as they arrive and give out any materials they need to complete before the session begins. This will eliminate any unnecessary distractions during instruction time.

Welcome

Teacher/Facilitator

Welcome to the (Church of Jesus)! This is our orientation session, which is another important step in your discipleship. In this session, we will discuss your decision to accept Christ as your Savior/join this assembly, the Discipleship Program of which you are now a part, your personal walk with Christ, and your participation in the programs of the church. You will also complete any membership documents and receive answers to any questions you may have. Let us stand and begin with prayer.

Pray and then sing: Come Follow Me

Come Follow Me

Come follow me; I know the way

That will lead you to the truth

Leave all behind for everything you need

The Lord will provide

Be my disciple I know the way

Be my disciple; follow me today

I hear His voice I know I'm lost

How I long to find the way

Here is my hand; I'll bear my cross

Lord give me strength I pray

I'm your disciple; you are the way

I'm your disciple; I'll follow you today

Play the Name Game (Self-Introductions)

The purpose of the Name Game is to encourage a sense of familiarity and bonding. In a large group/church setting, some people tend to feel overwhelmed. Playing this game will help those who may feel lost or insignificant to be comfortable.

Instruction

1. Ask each person to say his/her name(s).
2. Ask each person to say something about him/herself: job, hobbies, interests, etc.
3. Allow each person to state briefly why he/she joined the assembly

(Pay close attention to each person's self-disclosure. It will provide excellent points you can use to relate to each prospect. The skillful facilitator can personalize the lesson and apply it to each member of the class by name and circumstance during the teaching session).

N.B. Self-introductions also provide immediate feedback to the ministry of the church.

For example, they help to answer key questions:

a.   Who are the people being attracted to the church?

b.   Why were they drawn to the church?

c.   How were they introduced to the ministry?

d.   Where do they live in relation to the church location?

Self-introductions also give the teachers/facilitators opportunities to scrutinize the attendees, their motives, and their intents, which may need to be corrected by the session components. It is the responsibility of the facilitators to protect the flock from wolves in sheep's clothing.

Self-introductions are often where treacherous paws and claws are seen, instead of tender hooves, so pay close attention.

Inform

- Give information about the local church (a brief history). Where available, a video presentation of the history and development of the church may be shown

- Give information about the discipleship classes, stressing the importance of attendance

Give Biblical Perspective (see Appendix pg. 181)

- Review the "Roman Road" to reinforce the participants' understanding of salvation

- Share booklets, tracts, etc. that promote personal and spiritual growth (give/recommend booklets)

- Reinforce any decision by those attending to accept Christ and to join the assembly

- Answer any questions that may arise

Distribute the UNIT IA worksheet and ABCs of Salvation worksheets for submission to the UNIT IA Teacher/Facilitator (explain how to complete:

Prayer/Dismissal Tips

- Make sure the meeting room is reserved and set up appropriately in advance

- Have an adequate amount of handout materials ready for class

- Attendance and other data records should be at hand

- Arrive ahead of time and pray with other facilitators

- Work together as a team

- Collect all the required documents at the end of class

- Don't let one person's question, issue, or participation dominate the session
- Make referrals for persons with special needs that exceed orientation
- Preview the Table of Contents to encourage continuation and completion

2. THE ROMAN ROAD

The ancient Romans built long, straight roads throughout their dominions to facilitate travel and commerce, but mainly for the security of the Empire. Straight, long roads made it possible for sentries posted to see any advancing enemy groups from a far distance and to so avert attacks. No such image is envisioned here. The "Roman Road" in this case, refers to an evangelical tool — a way of outlining the plan of salvation using only the Scriptures found in the epistle to the Romans, hence the name.

Paul's letter to the church at Rome is an excellent treatise on God's plan of salvation for both Jews and Gentiles and is perhaps the most comprehensive in Scripture on the subject. Written by the apostle who met Jesus on a street called Straight, Paul's inspired letter to the brethren at Rome outlines the singular, straight, long road that leads to the kingdom of Christ and life eternal to all who will traverse that way by faith.

There are several advantages of the Roman road:

- The discipleship prospect is directed to one book in the Bible rather than being referred to several Scriptures throughout the Bible
- The unity of thought within one book makes it easy to outline pertinent truths
- It is easier to arrive at logical conclusions in a systematic way
- It is easier to remember the texts and relocate them, rather than trying to recall texts drawn from several books of the Bible
- It is a tested road used successfully by evangelists for many years
- It lends itself to each situation giving flexibility and versatility to the believers witnessing the gospel to those they seek to win over

With these advantages in mind, what follows is an outline that has been used successfully by soul winners over the years. Since there is no one set format, this version is presented here for the purposes of this study.

Introduction: The Bible

The teacher holds up the Bible in his/her hand before the class as the presentation is made.

The Bible will be our main text during our discipler studies. It is the most important and profound book that you will ever read. The information given here is better than any other text or media network source because of its supernatural nature. Unlike all other books or sources of information, the Bible predates, updates, and will postdate us. It is the Word of the LORD. Remember it was what we heard preached that led us here together; hence, we can see the profound effect the scriptures have had on our lives already. Therefore, it is vitally important that we become personally acquainted with the Bible and its message.

1.   **The Name**

Notice that Scripture is normally referred to as the Holy Bible but what does the word "Bible" mean? (Wait for answers and responses.)

Answer: The word "Bible" simply means book; it is derived from the Greek word *biblos*. Now, if it is a book, that means it is supposed to be read. That is the intended purpose of a book: to convey pertinent information from the mind of the author(s) to the mind of the reader(s) in the form of words, numbers, and other literary/artistic expressions.

Notice also, it is not just an ordinary book but it is called the Holy Book. What does holy mean? (Wait for answers and responses). "Holy" from the Hebrew word, Qadosh, refers to something or someone who is pure, clean, sanctified, set apart for divine use, and sinless. Ultimately, Qadosh refers to God who is most holy. Thus, if the meanings of these two words are put together, we derive that the Holy Bible is the book of God, a good book, a pure book, a clean book, a sanctified book, set apart for divine use. It was written by several different authors over thousands of years who were inspired by God's Holy Spirit to do so. These sacred writings document God's interactions with select men and women throughout history so that He may save mankind from sin, death, and the Devil.

Given all that, it warrants our reading particularly if it is God's book intended for us to read and understand. So let us open it to see what it says to us.

2.   **Table of Contents**

Remember that it is a book, albeit a holy book, so let us turn to the table of contents, which tells us what is listed inside. What do you see there? (Wait for answers and responses). As you have rightfully pointed out, we can see a list of the books of the Bible, their page numbers, divisions such as prophets, gospels, abbreviations, etc. depending on the type of Bible you have. The table of contents is there to help us locate what is within the Bible. Therefore, don't waste time flipping back and forth trying to find texts. Until you become familiar enough with it, look up the page number of the book and locate any text you are seeking.

3. Testaments

Notice the two principal divisions:

a. Old Testament

b. New Testament

What is a Testament? (Wait for answers and responses). Where in general do we often hear and use this term outside of church? (Wait for answers and responses). Most often, this term is used in legal matters such as giving testimony, testimonials, last will and testaments of the deceased, etc.

In that respect, a testament is a covenantal obligation undertaken between two parties. Because it is often in the form of a covenant, it has mutual obligations and considerations that are legally binding. It is a formal expression of a benefactor's intent to bestow benefits to a beneficiary from his/her estate. It is evidence of another's commitment and conviction.

From a theological standpoint, "testament" is an expression of God's declaration of His divine promises and will toward humanity whom He loves unconditionally. The concept is graphically expressed in the Hebrew word b'rit (covenant), which is often used synonymously for the word "testament." In the cutting of a covenant, both parties would offer animals that were "cut" in half. Both parties would make solemn promises to keep them on pain of death.

Applied in this context, the Bible may be viewed as God's account of sacred, gracious promises to His people and the obligations that His people have in reciprocity. Because God is faithful to His Word, it is essential that we are aware of what obligations are contained in the testaments (Old and New), which we have to honor. This is necessary lest we fall short of them and violate the terms of the covenants that apply to all humanity, but especially to us who are His people through Christ Jesus (Ephesians 1, 2; John 17).

The Bible ought to be read, studied, and understood to benefit from the divine blessing inherent in obeying it. Also, because God stands by His Word and will honor it above His holy name (Psalm 138:2), its instructions ought to be followed more than any other book, principle, philosophy, or theology that contradicts it. Failure to do so may deny us the immeasurable benefits it offers. Therefore, let us begin to acquaint ourselves with it.

4. Book of Books, Chapters, and Verses

You will notice that there are 39 books in the Old Testament and 27 in the New Testament totaling 66 books in all. These are the ones the leaders of the church throughout the centuries have confirmed to be authentic scriptures. Each book is divided into chapters and each chapter is divided into verses. Let us take a look at one of the best-known books in the Bible and examine its message again.

Text: Romans 3:10-18 (book, chapter#, verse(s))

Recall that the index will show you the page number for each book. Find the page where the book for the text given is located. Then turn to the chapter and the verses (ask a volunteer(s) to read the selected text above).

Some key observations:

The entire book of Romans is written to set out the basic tenets of the Christian faith. This text is God's assessment of the universal sinfulness of man.

- How many are righteous before God? "None...no not one."
- Notice the list of sinful behaviors that emanates from our being disobedient to God:
    a.   Lack of understanding
    b.   Not seeking God
    c.   Turning aside from the right path
    d.   Unprofitable living
    e.   Failing to do good
    f.   Deadly speech full of cursing and bitterness
    g.   Deceitful tongues
    h.   Feet that run swiftly to murder
    i.   Destructive miserable lifestyles
    j.   Devoid of peacefulness
    k.   Reverence for God is out of view

Now let us read verse 23 and make some observations:

- How many have sinned? All!
- What does "all" mean? It excludes no one and nothing, but includes everyone and everything; we are included here as guilty of sin!
- What does "sinned" mean? Acts of disobedience. Sin is anything we desire in our hearts and what we say or do that is displeasing to God; it is the transgression of His law.
- Our sinning causes us to fall short i.e. miss the mark of doing what would glorify Him (v.23).

Illustration

Johnny, a high school student achieves success and is on the honor roll at school; he is named valedictorian. He is featured in the newspapers. Imagine if you were his/her parent; would you not buy the newspaper to show it to your friends? Your child brought glory to you by his good works.

On the other hand, your child Jane is arrested for a crime and her picture is in the newspapers. Would you take the newspaper to work to show off or forward social media posting of it to your friends? Most likely you would not because she has fallen short of your standards and expectations.

Such is the case with us and God who created us and expects our obedience. There are consequences for sinful behaviors as we will see in the next stage on the Roman road.

Life or Death

Ask a volunteer to read Romans 6:23. Divide the class into two groups. Group 1 (left side of road) will focus on verse 23a and Group 2 (right side of road) on verse 23b.

Question: What are wages? (Directed to Group 1. Wait for responses).

Answer: Payment (for work rendered to another/company) salary, reward, compensation; result, earnings

Let us substitute those synonyms into the text for a clearer understanding (include suggestions from the groups):

 a. The payment for sin is death

 b. The salary for sin is death

 c. The reward for sin is death

 d. The compensation for sin is death

 e. The result of sin is death

 f. The earning for sin is death

Therefore, we die because of our misdeeds, not because God summarily destroyed us even though He could. If Johnny/Jane are rebellious against a parent: refusing to come home, staying out late with friends, hanging around bad influences who abuse drugs and alcohol, and commit crime, what is likely to happen to Johnny/Jane? The same is true for all who work in sin. They will die as a result and as a natural consequence.

Question: What is a gift? (Directed to Group 2. Wait for responses).

Answer: A present given to someone by another at his/her discretion. To the receiver, it has no price, but to the giver, it has a cost.

Notice that God's gift to everyone is eternal life. What a contrast to what we earned by our sinful works! Then, see who we may receive the gift courtesy of: "Jesus Christ our Lord." How so? The answer is found in the most known verse in the entire Bible:

> For God so loved the world, that he gave his only begotten Son, that whosoever believeth in him should not perish, but have everlasting life. (John 3:16 KJV)

We deserve death because of our sins, but God sacrificed His Son who willingly died in our place on the cross (extend hands to demonstrate crucifixion). In exchange, we live in His place and because He has eternal life we have the gift of His eternal life. Wow! What grace and salvation we find on the Roman road. Which side of the road is to be preferred?

With this, we must remember that a gift has to be received if it is to be of any value to the one for whom it is intended. Unless it is accepted, no matter how precious it is and how much it costs, the intent of the giver is in vain. Therefore we may ask ourselves, how does one receive the gift of God? Let us go on the next stage of the Roman road to find out.

Receiving the Gift

Text: Romans 10:9-13 (have volunteer(s) read)

The text shows us how the gift of eternal life is appropriated:

a.   Confess that Jesus Christ is Lord.

"Confess" in this context means to agree with God. It is essential to recognize that Jesus is the Christ i.e. the One God sent to save mankind from sin. Recognizing Jesus as Lord is seeing the One who alone has the power to save. He became the Lord of salvation because He not only died for the sins of the world paying the full penalty, but He rose again from the dead demonstrating His triumph over death and the grave comprehensively. As a result, He was "Declared to be the Son of God with power by the Spirit of holiness by the resurrection from the dead" (Romans 1:4 cf. 1 Corinthians 15). Hence, Jesus is the One who alone has all power and authority both in heaven and earth to save (Matthew 28:18).

b.   Believe in the heart that God has raised Him from the dead.

If Jesus did not rise from the dead, it would have been an indication that He was not righteous in the sight of God and hence, died for His own sins. Our sin debts would have remained unpaid (Romans 3:21-26 cf. I Corinthians 15:14-26)! We would only have hope on earth as we strive to emulate Him, but we would have no prospect of living with God eternally in heaven. Such a life would be one of misery and futility (1 Corinthians 15:12-19; Ecclesiastes 9:1-6).

Believing is putting confidence in the Word of God as the truth and acting on it accordingly. To believe is to trust the merits of what He says.

c.   You shall be saved!

When we put faith in God, He extends His grace to us so that we are forgiven and saved from condemnation for our sins. It does not matter if we are Jews (His covenantal people from whom Jesus came) or if we are Gentiles (all non-Jews). There is no distinction as long as we believe in the Son of God the Lord Jesus Christ. God pours out His grace richly to all (Romans 3 cf. Ephesians 2). Whoever calls on the name of the Lord shall be saved.

To be saved is to be delivered from all calamity: death, sickness, danger, enemies, distress, persecution, evil, bad circumstances etc. Therefore, our salvation must be understood to have begun now and will continue until we are taken out of this world into the new world to come (Revelation 21:1-7).

There are many other significant points along the Roman road we may stop to consider, but these are sufficient for us to understand and attain the salvation God intends for us. The most important question is whether you are on that path that leads to life eternal or on the road that leads to eternal damnation. In other words, are you here in this class because you have recognized your need to repent of your sins or for some other reason? Do you realize that Christ died in your place — the just for the unjust? Have you consciously asked God in your heart to forgive you of your sins that His gift of grace may be yours? Do you believe in the message of the gospel that Jesus is the Christ sent from God to save you? Have you confessed your sins and asked Him to save you? If you have done so sincerely then be assured that God keeps His word and has accepted you as His child as much as Christ His own beloved Son (Romans 8:12-17).

As a child of God, it is your responsibility to study God's Word so that your confidence grows and God's grace becomes a reality in your life day by day. This daily process of Christian living is called Christian discipleship, to which you will be introduced in this study. If you did not make a complete commitment to God, you will need to do so and may do so now before leaving this class. In this way, we may set out on the path of growth in our Christian faith together.

Ask for a show of hands of all who have already committed to being Christian disciples and those who need to do so. You may have facilitators minister separately to these as follows:

- Close the session with a prayer of salvation for all who are unsure
- Give an opportunity to others who may need further qualifications after class is dismissed
- Another facilitator could pray with those who are confident of salvation offering thanksgiving and blessings
- Distribute any handouts for the next class unit they will attend
- Remind them of the dates for the next class
- Dismissal and benediction

FOR FURTHER STUDY (OPTIONAL)

- Review Romans 5 and note the benefits of God's grace
- Review Romans 8 and note the privileges of those who are accepted in Christ
- Review Romans 9 & 11 and note the plan of salvation to both Jews and Gentiles
- Review Romans 12 and study your full commitment to God and your service to Him
- Review Romans 13, 14 & 15 and think through how a believer is to live in society and community with other believers and non-believers

Exercise A1.

1. Pray Psalm 51 aloud
2. Ask God to show you any sin(s) of which you need to repent
3. Ask God to lead you away from your sins
4. Memorize Psalm 139:23
5. Read the General Confession of the African-American Episcopal Church liturgy below
6. Meditate on it
7. Memorize it as your own prayer

3. A.M.E CONFESSION

Almighty God, Father of our Lord Jesus Christ, Maker of all things and judge of all men, we acknowledge and bewail our manifold sins and wickedness, which we from time to time most grievously have committed by thought, word, and deed against Your divine Majesty provoking most justly Your wrath and indignation against us. We do earnestly repent and are heartily sorry for these our misdoings; the remembrance of them is grievous unto us.

Have mercy upon us; have mercy upon us, most merciful Father for Your Son our Lord Jesus Christ' sake. Forgive us all that is past and grant that we may ever hereafter serve and please You in the newness of life, to the honor and glory of Your name, through Jesus Christ our Lord. Amen.[xv]

---

xv   The Doctrines and Disciplines of The African American Church (1817)

4. WESTMINSTER CONFESSION ON REPENTANCE

Chapter XV

Of Repentance unto Life

I. Repentance unto life is an evangelical grace, the doctrine whereof is to be preached by every minister of the Gospel, as well as that of faith in Christ.

II. By it, a sinner, out of the sight and sense not only of the danger, but also of the filthiness and odiousness of his sins, as contrary to the holy nature, and righteous law of God; and upon the apprehension of His mercy in Christ to such as are penitent, so grieves for, and hates his sins, as to turn from them all unto God, purposing and endeavouring to walk with Him in all the ways of His commandments.

III. Repentance is not to be rested in, as any satisfaction for sin or any cause of the pardon thereof, which is the act of God's free grace in Christ, yet it is of such necessity to all sinners, that none may expect pardon without it.

IV. As there is no sin so small, but it deserves damnation, so there is no sin so great, that it can bring damnation upon those who truly repent.

V. Men ought not to content themselves with a general repentance, but it is every man's duty to endeavor to repent of his particular sins, particularly.

VI. As every man is bound to make private confession of his sins to God, praying for the pardon thereof; upon which, and the forsaking of them, he shall find mercy; so he that scandelizeth his brother, or the Church of Christ, ought to be willing, by a private or public confession and sorrow for his sin, to declare his repentance to those that are offended; who are thereupon to be reconciled to him, and in love to receive him.[xvi]

Discuss any observations you make of these two confessions above.

ADDITIONAL PERSONAL REFLECTION

a. What do you believe about the gospel message you have heard?

b. Do you believe in the message of the gospel in principle only or have you surrendered your will to the will of God as expressed in the gospel message?

c. What do you see in your personal conduct that needs to be changed in accordance with your new found faith?

---

xvi   Westminister Confession Chapter xv (1646)

d.   What new fruit have you observed in your life? (peace, joy, etc.)

e.   What have you done differently as a result of your decision to follow Jesus?

Ask God to bring to mind anyone you may have sinned against. Pray for an opportunity to ask the person for forgiveness and make amends wherever possible. Be prepared for possible rejection, but remember you are not responsible for the person's lack of forgiveness only your lack of asking for it.

NOTE: You may need professional advice in some areas before you attempt reconciliation with anyone you may have hurt or are hurting now. Therefore, be prayerful and careful not to rush or force situations to satisfy your need for forgiveness. Allow godly counsel. Ask the class facilitators for possible referrals to professional help/service.

BIBLIOGRAPHY

i. *Theological Wordbook of The Old Testament* (electronic ed.) (490). Chicago: Moody Press. Harris, R. L., Archer, G. L., & Waltke, B. K. (1999, c1980).

ii. Vines Complete Expository of The Old and New Testament Words, Thomas Nelson Publishers 1996 (pg. 275-276)

iii. Ibid, pg. 525

iv. Ibid, pg. 61

v. The Septuagint Version of The Old Testament in Greek

vi. Harris, Robert Laird; Archer, Gleason Leonard: Waltke, Bruce K.: *Theological Wordbook of The Old Testament.* electronic ed. Chicago: Moody Press, 1999, c1980, S.

vii. Ibid

viii. Synder, Howard A, The Community of the King, IVP, 1977

ix. Harris, R. Laird; Archer, Gleason Leonard; Waltke, Bruce K.: *Theological Wordbook of the Old Testament.* electronic ed. Chicago: Moody Press, 1999, c1980, S. 215

x. Wikipedia

xi. Theology of the Older Testament, pg. 434

xii. Ibid

xiii. Nepho Gerson Laoly, The Tithe (Web Posting, May 8th, 2012)

xiv. Bryan Green, The Power of Cooperative Evangelism, (EMIS)

xv. The Doctrines and Disciplines of the African American Church (1817)

xvi. Westminister Confession Chapter xv (1646)

www.ingramcontent.com/pod-product-compliance
Lightning Source LLC
Chambersburg PA
CBHW062044090426

42740CB00016B/3018

* 9 7 8 1 5 6 2 2 9 3 7 5 8 *